Methods of
Teaching English
to
Arab Students

Najat Al-Mutawa

Taiseer Kailani

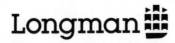

Addison Wesley Longman Limited,
Edinburgh Gate, Harlow,
Essex, CM20 2JE, England
and Associated Companies throughout the world.

First published 1989
Fourth impression 1996

ISBN 0 582 03648 8

Set in Plantin Light

Printed in China
PPC/04

Contents

List of Abbreviations

EFL	English as a Foreign Language
ELT	English Language Teaching
ESL	English as a Second Language
ESOL	English for Speakers of Other Languages
FL	Foreign Language
L1	First Language/Mother Tongue
L2	Second/Foreign Language
RP	Received Pronunciation
TEFL	Teaching English as a Foreign Language
TESOL	Teaching English to Speakers of Other Languages

Preface

English is becoming the first foreign language throughout the Arab World. It also enjoys important status in North Africa where French is the predominant foreign language. English is being widely used in the fields of business, industry, technology, politics, education, medicine and various other professional fields. Consequently, there is a need for teaching it communicatively. Unfortunately, most of the books and articles dealing with this subject are the product of foreign linguists. They often overlook the issues and problems encountered in Arab countries.

This book attempts to discuss the difficulties that influence the teaching of English in Arab schools. It aims to familiarize the Arab teacher of English with key aspects of methodology. It also suggests strategies and techniques through which the elements and communicative skills of the language can be taught. It pays special attention to the conditions and factors influencing the effectiveness of the teaching of the language in our schools.

The book is intended for practising and prospective EFL teachers, college students majoring in English and the general interested reader. It presents many ideas on using approaches and strategies, substance and techniques for teaching sound, grammar, vocabulary and cultural subsystems. Suggestions for developing the communication skills, namely listening, speaking, reading and writing are also included. In addition, a wide variety of communication activities has been incorporated for teaching discrete linguistic features, and communicative abilities.

The book is divided into five major parts.

PART ONE presents an overview of the status of English in the Arab world.

PART TWO reviews methods and approaches to foreign language teaching and learning.

PART THREE focuses on specific techniques for teaching the language, its sound system, its vocabulary, its grammar and its cultural aspects.

PART FOUR presents techniques and suggestions for developing the communicative skills of listening, speaking, reading and writing.

PART FIVE deals with issues and procedures directly concerned with what goes on in the classroom and discusses motivational variables in foreign language learning. A comprehensive bibliography is also provided for interested readers.

The book could not have been written without the help of many colleagues and students. We wish to express our thanks to all of them.

Najat Al-Mutawa   *Taiseer Kailani*

Part One

Introductory
Background

Chapter One

Some Basic Principles

1.1

Definitions

English as a first language: This refers to native speakers of the English-speaking world who learn the language as their mother tongue. It exists, in those countries, in different forms and varieties. For example, British English has distinctive aspects of pronunciation and usage compared with American English. Even within these varieties many dialects can be found.

In a first language situation, a child usually internalizes the system of its mother tongue at an early stage. The process of learning is natural and full of variety. Motivation is strong in the young learner as he is prompted by inner drive. Language is a key to the discovery of the outside world and to his cognitive development. The language he acquires surrounds him from birth and this linguistic environment constantly reinforces his learning.

English as a second language: A second language is one which has some specific functions within a multilingual society or minority groups, and is learned after the mother tongue. As a second language, English is taught in conditions where there is some reinforcement from the child's immediate environment and the language is used extensively in everyday life. The language usually functions as the lingua franca, i.e. the normal medium of instruction and communication. It is also used as the official language of government institutions, of commercial and industrial organizations and of the mass media. This situation prevails in multilingual communities like Canada, South Africa, Tanzania, Ghana, Nigeria, Malaysia, India and Pakistan. It is thus essential that the individual learns the target language in order to be equipped with an instrument of communication between members of different communities. Motivation to learn the language remains strong as in first language acquisition, but it is both instrumental and integrative.[1] That is, while the individual feels that the needs of his

---

[1] Instrumental motivation refers to the pragmatic or utilitarian value of learning a second language. On the other hand, integrative motivation means learning the language to know more about another community's culture with the aim of integrating with it (see Gardner and Lambert 1972).

immediate linguistic environment are met through the medium of the mother tongue, he cannot communicate with natives outside his community without the second language.

English as a foreign language: A foreign language is one which has no internal function in the learner's country. It is learnt in order to communicate with native speakers or interlanguage users of the foreign language. In this setting, as in the Arab world, English has no official status. Learning of the foreign language is confined to the classroom. That is, the language is taught and used in schools. Normally, there is little, if any, reinforcement outside the school. The language is learnt like other subjects in the school curriculum for operational purposes. Unlike the first two learning situations, motivation for learning the target language in this context is not high. This is especially the case in the early stages because young children are still unaware of their individual needs and interests. Motivation depends largely on the teacher, the method, the language activities, the textbooks and the classroom situation.

1.2

The place of English in the Arab world

English holds an eminent place in most of the Arab countries owing to the traditional relationship maintained with the English-speaking world. There are extensive commercial, cultural and other interdependent activities with the United Kingdom and the United States. This results in a favourable attitude towards the language and consequently a strong drive to learn it. This status has recently been enhanced by the rapid growth of science and technology.

There is, however, a paradox in the use of English. Although its position seems pre-eminent across the Arab world, the language remains superficial or even irrelevant to the majority of the population, especially in rural areas where Arabic is the sole medium of communication. Culturally, Arabic is used as the vehicle of writing, instruction and correspondence both in government and civic institutions.

Nevertheless, English is the most widely used means of international communication. Arabs need to learn English to communicate with native speakers of English as well as with interlanguage users of English abroad or within the Arab world. Thus English is often used as a lingua franca when an Arab engineer, for example, wants to confer with an Indian or Korean colleague. Even in North African countries where French is regarded as the second language, English teaching occupies a prominent place in the school curriculum. The teaching of English, in the Arab world, is constantly emphasized because of its universality and the sophisticated and advanced culture of the English-speaking world. Many Arab countries send an increasing number of students and academics to the USA and Britain for undergraduate and postgraduate studies. The students normally benefit a great deal through integrating themselves with the people, the culture and the modern technology.

However, the need for English varies from one Arab state to another, depending on the degree of relationship with the English-speaking countries. English constitutes, throughout the Arab world, the main instrument of data processing, computer applications, telecommunications, foreign trade, and banking, and is the medium of instruction at technical institutions and scientific faculties. There are also other spheres of life in which English is employed, such as travelling abroad, sports and medicine. The reasons for learning English in the Arab world, may be summarized as follows:

(a) The political, cultural and economic relationship between the Arab world and the English-speaking countries creates the need for educated Arabs to be competent in English.

(b) The achievements of the English-speaking world in the fields of education, art, science and technology enhance willingness among Arabs to learn English. Through it, they acquaint themselves with the civilization and cultural advancement of the Western world.

(c) Widespread exposure to English mass media such as radio and TV programmes, cine and video films, books, periodicals, journals and other publications, motivates the desire to learn the language for enjoyment and cultural purposes.

(d) English is the first international language of commerce, telecommunications, aviation, computer services, science and technology.

(e) Command of the language enables one to appreciate the work of other people and the way they think, since it is the major vehicle by means of which every branch of human thought is discussed, translated and made available.

(f) In travelling abroad, English is very helpful in communication. A traveller who can speak English will usually find others who can understand him wherever he may go (see Broughton 1978, Ch. 1).

(g) English is a means of communication between non-native speakers. It is used as a lingua franca through which one can converse or interact with varied people, not necessarily native speakers of English.

(h) A good command of English is an essential requirement for careers, especially at the senior levels.

(i) English is a world language and the common property of all cultures. It helps one to understand other peoples and their way of life.

To sum up, Arab learners of English are, on the whole, instrumentally motivated. This should be taken into consideration when planning or designing an English syllabus. Consequently, EFL teachers should be aware of their pupils' motives for learning English and reinforce that motivation in their teaching approach, materials and practices.

1.3
English as a School Subject

English teaching has a dominant position in Arab schools and is relatively well established. English has occupied a prominent place in the school curriculum for at least half a century. It is taught in all government schools as a compulsory subject and as the first foreign language. For example in Kuwait the teaching of English starts in the first grade of the intermediate school at the rate of six to seven 45-minute periods per week. Its teaching is continued up to the end of the secondary stage; pupils thus spend eight years studying English. And upon going to university or technical college, they study English either for general or for academic purposes. The language is also used as the medium of instruction in many private schools.

English in state schools is granted the same value and prestige as the mother tongue. Its teaching has always been concerned with developing the pupils' ability to communicate. It aims at making learners understand and use the language in its spoken and written forms within a particular cultural context, and to build up the pupils' communicative competence so that they can use it in their future life.

In the process of learning the language, Arab pupils are dependent on the teacher and on the input that the classroom provides, since English is not used outside the school. It is only in the classroom setting that they can learn English or reinforce the skills and knowledge learnt. However, pupils are sometimes exposed to such situations as watching English-speaking films, travelling or shopping where they can practise their newly acquired language.

1.4

English Teaching Goals and Objectives

1. *General goals:* These refer to the purposes of English education and to the achievements of English learners after eight years of English schooling. They are often put into the form of expectations on the part of the learner, and they can be summed up as follows:

   (a) The teaching of English aims at developing the pupils' proficiency in understanding and using the language in spoken and written forms. The secondary-school learner is expected to understand, speak, read and write English with a measure of ease, finesse and discrimination.

   (b) At the same time, English teaching should improve the pupils' competence so that they can communicate in those situations where they have to use English rather than Arabic. The secondary-school leavers should have developed the ability to use the language as a practical means of communication and self-expression.

   (c) The teaching of English should also enable pupils to become well informed about the life and culture of the countries which use English as a means of expression. This broad aim means that after eight years of English learning, pupils should be cultivated, useful and perceptive citizens so that they can establish a solid foundation for international understanding.

These general objectives of English education generally correspond to ELT aims in other Arab countries where English is also taught as a first foreign language.

2. *Specific objectives:* The behavioural objectives are defined by the English syllabus for each stage of learning. They are classified in relation to the cognitive, affective and psychomotor domains. Thus, the receptive skills (listening and reading) and the productive skills (speaking and writing) are specified and graded according to these taxonomies or classifications. It is stated clearly what performance is expected from the pupil at the end of each school year regarding each area of learning. However, these general objectives stress knowledge of the components of communicative competence. The aim is to develop the pupil's ability to communicate appropriately in English. He should be able to understand the words of others, spoken or written, and be understood in return. It is thus necessary to

review the components of communicative competence since each of them stands for ELT objectives that should be achieved throughout the different stages of English teaching.

1.5
Components of Communicative Competence

The conceptual model in Fig. 1 specifies the components of communicative competence. Linguistic knowledge is the core of the wheel and this inner wheel shows the relationship between the components, whereas the outer wheel, fluency, is the outcome of the learning process. These components are illustrated as follows:[1]

1. Linguistic competence, i.e. knowledge
2. Pragmatic competence
3. Strategic competence
4. Socio-cultural competence
5. Fluency

1.6
Central Determinants

As shown in the conceptual model of communicative competence, there are several factors on which the integrated components rest. However, we shall refer here only to those areas that relate directly to the process of building up communicative competence. The remaining factors will be discussed in subsequent chapters.[2]

1. The pupil

Empirical evidence has shown that there is a significant link between achievement or success in EFL learning and the pupil's willingness to learn. That is, satisfactory results are produced by motivated pupils irrespective of their sex and age. Developing communicative competence requires an active contribution from the pupil and an ability to learn. The pupils should be able, therefore, to take full part in interaction in the classroom, react to and discuss texts, and participate in group discussions and pair/group work activities. Otherwise they will be unable to develop their communicative competence.

2. The EFL teacher

English language teaching is qualitatively different from other types of teaching, because special qualifications and training are required for the EFL teacher. He must have (a) adequate proficiency in all the areas of communicative competence; (b) metacommunicative knowledge, i.e. knowledge of rules governing linguistic forms, namely grammar, pronunciation and vocabulary; (c) socio-cultural knowledge; (d) processes of learning and communicative practices; and (e) professional skills. A teacher who is communicatively incompetent will be unable to teach English communicatively. Consequently he will not succeed in giving his pupils a good command of English.

---

[1] For further details see Appendix I
[2] See Chapter 3 and Part Five, Procedures and techniques.

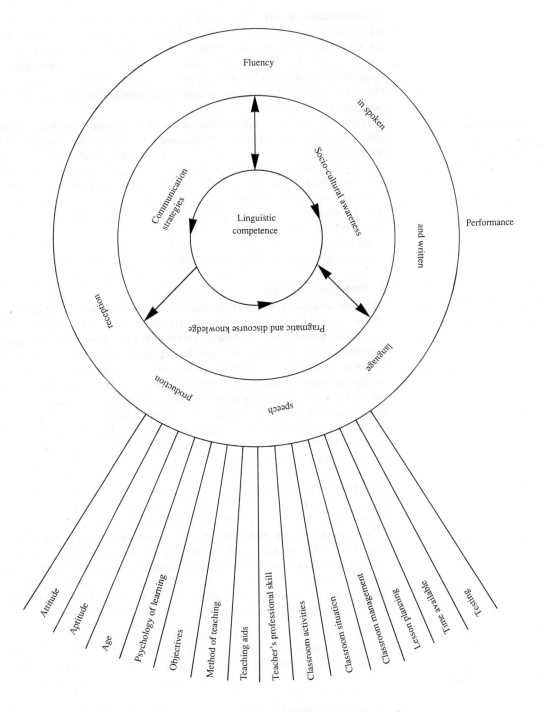

Factors influencing effectiveness of English Language teaching/learning

Fig. 1: Components of communicative competence

3. The method of teaching

ELT methodology varies from one Arab country to another. Some countries are employing a structural approach or a modified audio-lingual method. Other countries are still using traditional methods, and some others are adopting an eclectic strategy incorporating features of different approaches. However, since 1980 the Arab countries in the Gulf area have adopted the communicative approach.

This new methodology (often called the notional-functional method) advocates teaching of the foreign language in terms of language functions, rather than in terms of grammar or vocabulary. It also emphasizes the conscious acquisition of the language as a meaningful system and as a creative process. The method stresses communicative activities in the classroom right from the beginning of learning the language. It emphasizes activities like role-playing, problem-solving, simulations, dialogues, small group interaction and language games. The aim is to practise aspects of linguistic competence, to develop the pupils' pragmatic and strategic competence and at the same time to build up their productive and receptive skills.

4. The teaching materials

Methods and materials are inseparable because the former is the application of the latter. Appropriate teaching materials are, therefore, required to help pupils to communicate, to interact and to practise the language by means of communicative activities and drills.[1] Such material should be natural, realistic and based on the concept of communicative methodology which views language learning as a thinking process. It is important to have authentic materials since pupils get real satisfaction by making some sense out of real-life language. Furthermore, the teaching materials should offer pupils an opportunity to practise the study skills and to develop the receptive and productive skills through language use, not through knowledge of linguistic rules.

5. The classroom environment

Classroom environment refers to all physical objects like chairs, desks, tables, illumination, recorders, projectors, blackboard, posters, wall-pictures and other equipment that is available in the classroom. The term involves also how these objects are employed in the teaching–learning process. The provision of adequate physical facilities in the classroom situation is essential for effective communicative competence. The classroom should be equipped with all the tools and teaching materials necessary for the activities that the teacher is expected to carry out. Thus the classroom should be

(a) Pleasant and attractive in appearance and well-organized.
(b) Well-ventilated and air conditioned, especially in hot areas where pupils and teachers would have to work under severe conditions. Hot weather slows down the process of teaching and distracts the pupils' attention from the lesson activities.
(c) Spacious enough to stimulate pupil–pupil interaction, to carry out communicative activities or group discussions and to keep teaching

[1] Teaching materials include: pupil's book, pupil's workbook, pupil's handwriting books, teacher's book, audio-visual aids, language learning activities, games and practices.

materials inside it to be used when needed. The class should be of appropriate size (not exceeding 30 pupils) so that the teacher can have a chance to cater for different groups, special cases or individual differences, and the pupils can feel free to participate actively in the learning process. The smaller the size of the class, the more co-operative the pupils are, and the stronger the interpersonal relations are.

With such facilities competence is feasible. Otherwise the process of teaching will remain just chalk and talk and the learning mere reciting.

1.7

Linguistics and Language Teaching

In a general sense, language is a complex medium of communication; it consists of a number of linked systems of which the system of vocal sounds (i.e. the spoken form) is of primary importance. The other components are words, grammar and meaning systems. They are often referred to as phonetics, lexis, syntax and semantics respectively. How these systems function is the concern of linguistics. This science, however, has various branches which deal with language differently. The major branches are:

Historical linguistics which describes the changes that a language has undergone through centuries (e.g. old English, middle English and modern English). It also traces back in time the relations between languages and their families, such as the Indo-European family or Anglo-Saxon English.

Comparative linguistics which is concerned with the study of languages in their written forms.

Descriptive linguistics which analyses the phonological and grammatical aspects of language in use.

Psycholinguistics which is concerned with 'the study of the relationship between linguistic and psychological behaviour. Psycholinguists study first and second language acquisition; the relationship between language and cognition, or thought; and how humans store and retrieve linguistic information, or verbal processing' (Davis 1986).

Sociolinguistics which is concerned with the study of language as it is actually used in real situations. That is linguistic knowledge as well as communicative competence, as a learner 'acquires knowledge of sentences, not only as grammatical, but also as appropriate. He or she acquires competence as to when to speak, when not, and as to what to talk about with whom, when, where, in what manner' (Pride and Holness 1972, pp. 276–8).

Applied linguistics which refers to the deployment of significant linguistic findings to language data. This is closely associated with language teaching as it makes use of linguistic principles in solving problems or answering questions of how to learn, say, the structure of one language, or the sound system as demonstrated by descriptive linguistics.

1.8

Linguistic Principles

Theoretical linguistics investigates language as a science to describe how it works. It suggests implications that can be drawn from the main findings and principles related to the nature and workings of language.

The following are some of the relevant linguistic principles:

Language is basically oral: this principle implies that language is mainly an oral activity (i.e. speech) and writing is an attempt at representing language. The English system is inaccurate as an alphabet. For example, some sounds are represented by two letters, e.g. *ph* for *f*, some letters represent no sound, e.g. the final *e* in *wide* and *horse*. The same letter or letters can stand for more than one sound. For example, in *busy, bus, possess*, the letter 's' is pronounced /z/ in the first word, and /s/ in the second, while in the third word the first 'ss' is pronounced /z/ and the second 'ss' /s/.

Language is systematic and learnable: language is a complex inter-woven system. Its elements are systematic at all levels: phonetic, phonemic, morphemic, morphological, syntactic and semantic levels. An important implication of the systematic nature of language is that the acquisition of a system enables a speaker to generate an infinite number of grammatically correct sentences.

Language is a means of communication: since language is an important instrument of communication, its teaching should aim at developing a communicative competence in learners. This can be achieved through providing the learners with learning activities to practise communication with one another in a meaningful and natural way.

Language changes: to match the changing social needs. Such variations are clearly manifested in vocabulary change.

Language is arbitrary: (see Titone 1968) There is no logical reason why a certain segment of the language behaves as it does. For example, the plural of house is houses and the plural of mouse is mice. The principle has the following implications for teaching:
(a) Reasoning about language forms or structure is often useless with beginners. Explanations are helpful only with advanced learners.
(b) Constant practice and intensive work are often the best way to master language.

Language has form and meaning: form can be studied scientifically and it can be described accurately. However, meaning does not lend itself to scientific study easily. The implication is that meaning of forms (spoken or written) can be determined by the situation or context in which they are said or used.

1.9

Language Knowledge

Knowing a language is not only a knowledge of correct grammar but also includes a knowledge of its use in an appropriate manner. The implication of this principle is that a foreign language programme should teach both use and usage, that is knowledge of the language system and its realization in contexts of use.

1.10

Language Acquisition and Language Learning

The term 'Language Acquisition' is often used to denote the process which results in the knowledge of one's mother tongue in normal conditions. The process is natural and starts from infancy at the time when the child is acquiring knowledge and skills from the immediate environment before formal schooling (see Hawkins 1981).

'Language Learning', on the other hand, is used in a foreign language context, that is in learning a second language. The process of learning here proceeds in a quite different way. Here the learning is systematic and gradual. It usually takes place in artificial settings at school where the learner is exposed to the language for short periods. The learning process usually starts at the age of ten plus when the system of the native language (i.e. the linguistic performance of the mother tongue) has already become established.

1.11

Psychological Principles

The following principles are often referred to by foreign language teachers. They are related to the empiricist approach of structural linguistics. This views language acquisition as habit formation, a process of stimulus, response and reinforcement.

Language learning is habit formation: (see Diller 1978, Ch. 2) This implies that learning a foreign language cannot be done in a matter of days or months. Constant practice and repetition over a relatively long period of time is needed. It also implies that learning a foreign language does not involve the mere accumulation of facts, but the assimilation of patterns of behaviour. The teacher, therefore, should never confuse language learning with the memorization of words and rules of grammar.

Language learning is the acquisition of a set of skills: The skills may be divided into two categories (i) Receptive, which are listening and reading and (ii) Productive skills, writing and speaking.

Since recognition precedes and is easier than production, pupils should start with listening comprehension before proceeding to write or speak.

The learning of a second language involves some mother tongue interference: The teaching of a foreign language can benefit a great deal from contrastive studies that point out similarities and differences in the two languages.

Language learning is accomplished through exposing the learner to a model: This principle stresses the importance of the model for imitation purposes. The teacher is the chief available model in most language learning situations; therefore, he ought to have a native-like fluency in the foreign language he is teaching. If such a teacher is not available, tape-recordings of native speakers can be used as models to be imitated.

Language learning is basically enjoyable: As children communicate they feel relief and enjoyment. Consequently, language learning should be made as pleasant as possible. This can be achieved by language learning activities such as games, classroom discussions, interviews, dialogues, role-playing, and problem-solving.

Language learning is both an individual and a social process: It is individual because the speaker or writer projects himself as a distinct person or writer in what he says or writes. It is social in the sense that language use enables the user to get along with others. In other words, it is process of interaction. Therefore, foreign language teaching should provide the learners with ample opportunity to work and use the language together in realistic and meaningful situations.

1.12

Techniques, Methods and Approaches

It is worthwhile discussing briefly the difference between these three aspects which are often used in foreign language teaching. A technique is the procedure used by the teacher in the classroom. In other words, it is what the teacher actually does in the classroom to implement a method which is, in turn, consistent with an approach.

A method, on the other hand, is the application of the detailed aspects of an approach. It consists of a number of techniques used in a systematic way to achieve the aim of language learning. The method comprises the lesson plan, the syllabus, the textbook, other teaching materials and the number of teaching periods. It also includes decisions made about language teaching outside the classroom. All these components should be in harmony with the basic tenets of the selected approach. However, the teacher is not bound by these two aspects, namely techniques and methods. He can utilize other teaching strategies pertinent to his approach in order to ensure efficient learning.

The term 'approach' refers to principles or assumptions underlying the process of language teaching and learning. For example, one of the assumptions underlying descriptive linguistics is that language is a set of habits, i.e. habit formation which is acquired by the process of stimulus, response and reinforcement. This principle is translated into 'mim-mem' (mimicry-memorization) and pattern practice. (This is the method.) How the teacher manipulates 'mim-mem' pattern practice is the technique.

It is clear from the foregoing that these three aspects are interdependent. They form a hierarchical system with the approach at the top followed by method and technique respectively. However, different approaches may share the same techniques or even the same methods which, in turn, may also share the same techniques. Although the concept of approach means certain theoretical beliefs or principles (e.g. the behaviourist approach, or the communicative approach), the term is often used in the sense of method especially when talking informally. For example, an efficient teacher always varies his approach when teaching classes of different abilities. This does not mean that the teacher will change his theoretical beliefs for each type of class. But he varies his methods and techniques to meet the different levels of his classes.

Part Two

Methods and Approaches to Foreign Language Teaching

Chapter Two

Foreign Language Teaching Methods and Approaches

Teaching

2.1

The Grammar–Translation Method (Indirect Method)

The grammar–translation method was widely used until two or three decades ago. Some of its characteristics are still present in most foreign language classrooms. The method was originally used to teach Latin, a language which was not taught for everyday communication. However the method was gradually generalized to teach living or modern languages such as English, French, etc. It has been used by teachers of English for about a hundred years.

As a discipline, this method aims at mastery of the general rules governing the written language and translation from and into the foreign language. To help pupils achieve such aims, linguists and grammarians prescribe the whole grammar of the language according to certain criteria – what is right and what is wrong. That is, they are concerned with making rules on how people ought to speak and write in conformity with some agreed standards. No attention is paid to practical mastery of the language, as the method does not concern itself with how pupils learn the language or how they actually use it. The main concern is linguistic. Thus students studying classical languages (Latin and Greek) had to spend their time in defining the parts of speech, and in memorizing conjugations, declensions and rules of grammar of these languages. They were also required to translate literary selections making heavy use of dictionaries in order to explain the meaning of the foreign language vocabulary in the mother tongue.

Pupils learning English according to this method have to learn by heart grammatical rules and tables of conjugations, and have to translate with the help of a dictionary.

The main limitations underlying the grammar–translation method can be summarized as follows:

(a) The method aims at knowing the grammar of the language which provides the rules for putting words together. Long elaborate explanations of the intricacies of grammar are given, and instructions often focus on the form and inflection of words.

(b) It does not set out rules enabling the learner to construct systematically correct complex sentences. The pupils are often trained in artificial forms of language when practising the rules.

(c) It takes little account of present-day language usage. Instead, it imposes norms generally derived from the language of the great authors of previous centuries. The textbooks contain long extracts from great writers chosen for intellectual content and which aim at providing the pupil with a wide literary vocabulary.

(d) It emphasizes the written language at the expense of the functional nature of the language and of how it is used to convey social functions such as requesting, greeting, expressing feelings, introducing people or showing attitudes, etc. Communicative skills are neglected since the stress is on knowing rules and exceptions.

(e) Pupils practise reading for the sake of memorizing a number of vocabulary items and for translation.

(f) Because the approach concerns itself primarily with the written language, and neglects speaking skills, little attention is given to accurate pronunciation and intonation.

(g) Much vocabulary is taught in the form of lists of separate words. However the teaching of vocabulary is inadequate because the choice of words is not made on a scientific basis. Words are used in sentences to illustrate grammatical rules and are presented out of context.

(h) As for the technique of teaching, this is done mostly in the native language through which the teacher explains the words and structures of the foreign language. Such over-usage of the native language reduces the time available for practice in the target language. Moreover, the technique of giving definitions, rules and explanations very frequently makes the process of teaching boring and of little benefit to the pupils.

In such a teaching situation, the pupils' role is largely passive. There are two reasons for this. The functional and social nature of the language is disregarded in the grammar–translation method, and the training is often carried out by drills taken from classical texts which usually have nothing to do with the pupils' interests and needs. The student learns more about how the language works than about how to *use* the language in a communicative way.

However, this method is still in use in many educational systems. As for the Arab world, a purely grammar–translation method has not been used for teaching although some aspects of it have been used. What happened, until the sixties, was that teachers were employing procedures and techniques drawn from this method, the Direct method and the Reading method. Thus grammar and translation teaching went hand in hand with language use through demonstrations, dramatization and reading silently and reading aloud. This situation continued to prevail until the audio-lingual method and the communicative approach emerged in the last two decades.

2.2

The Direct Method

As explained in the preceding section, the grammar–translation method could not be of help to those who want to speak the foreign language with a reasonable degree of fluency. In order to overcome this shortcoming, the Direct method was developed for the teaching of foreign languages. It became popular throughout the early years of the twentieth century. By 'Direct' is meant teaching in the foreign language, without use of the mother tongue. The theory, however, was based on the assumption that learning a foreign language is very much like learning one's mother tongue, i.e. 'that exposing the language impresses it perfectly upon the learner's mind' (Lado 1961, p. 5). This belief has proved to be false because learning the native language in childhood does not assure the acquisition of a foreign language adequately in adulthood. Moreover, language acquisition in childhood is a trait while language learning in adulthood is a skill. Psychologists believe that unless the first language is acquired by early childhood, the capacity to acquire any human language will become meagre and limited. In contrast, the learning of a second language is not restricted to people of a particular age. Nonetheless, the Direct method was received with enthusiasm by foreign language teachers in Europe and the United States. The main features underlying it can be summed up as follows:

(a) It gives priority to speech and oral skills, and rejects memorization of conjugations, declensions and rules of grammar. At the same time it rejects the pupils' mother tongue as it considers translation a useless activity in teaching a foreign language; therefore the meaning of concrete or abstract words and sentences is given through dramatization, demonstration or pointing at objects without the use of the mother tongue.

(b) Grammatical rules are not taught. They are acquired unconsciously through practical use (i.e. intensive listening and imitation). That is to say rule generalization comes after experience.

(c) The new material is presented orally. Thus words and patterns are taught through direct association with actions, dialogues, situations, objects or pictures. 'Mim-mem' technique is also used. Pupils memorize selected foreign language sentences, short dialogues, expressions and songs after imitation. The mother tongue is never used in all these activities. The preferred type of exercise is a series of questions based on these activities and answered in the target language. Verbs are systematically conjugated.

(d) Reading and writing are deferred for months. Reading aloud is done in the early stages and pronunciation is emphasized. Advanced learners read literature for comprehension and pleasure; literary texts are not analysed grammatically.

(e) The culture of the target language is also taught inductively.

Many techniques and procedures are developed to make this method more effective in foreign language teaching and learning. For example, statements are demonstrated with actions and pupils repeat both the language model and the actions as in this sentence: 'I'm standing up. I'm going to the window. I'm looking at the traffic in the street. I see a boy riding on a bicycle,' etc.

Such sequential exercise is usually followed by related questions such as What are you doing? Where are you going? What are you looking at? What can you see? What is the boy doing? etc., or questions such as Where is he going? Where did he go? etc.

This is a typical process of teaching and learning in accordance with this method. However, such exercises have failed to achieve decisive results, or authentic learning on the part of the pupil because all the language activities are, in general, related to the classroom and not connected with real life situations. In other words, they do not prepare the learners to use the foreign language for communication. The teachers do not think of pupils using the language outside the classroom.

This method has been criticized for being time-consuming and the least direct approach. Its insistence on giving the meaning of words and structures through dramatization, demonstration or association without resorting to the mother tongue has led to the using of roundabout techniques which are time-wasting. This process might be successful with concrete sentences but fails with abstract words. Using the native language, therefore, in some instances ensures that the required meaning is comprehended in addition to the fact that it saves time. A further advantage, as already mentioned, is that valuable learning time is saved. Moreover, the method requires, among other things, for its proper application, a highly competent teacher who is endowed with fluency in the foreign language and adequate knowledge of its techniques. It also requires a large number of class hours since most of the work is done in the classroom. In addition, the direct method suffers from lack of selection, gradation and controlled presentation of contents. Consequently pupils are never clear about what they are studying.

It is clear that the two foregoing methods, namely the Indirect and the Direct, are rather extreme. On the one hand, the chief purpose of the grammar–translation method is to develop an ability to translate while the spoken language is neglected. The Direct method, on the other hand, lays heavy emphasis on the oral aspects of the language and intensive speech practice. Yet it discards the use of translation. A new method known as the Reading method emerged in the thirties.

2.3
The Reading Method

The method was known in the Arab world as the West's method. It became popular during the period between 1930 and 1960 when it was replaced by the audio-lingual method. However, some variations of the Reading method such as oral, silent, selective, free and comprehension readings are still practised in English classes.

The method aims at achieving an intensive reading skill for the purposes of comprehension, vocabulary acquisition and grammatical rules. On the other hand, the Reading method aims at extensive reading where learners read on their own special readers which are graded in order gradually to develop their reading abilities. Translation is, however, discouraged. Instead, learners are trained to deduce the meaning of words from the context. That is, their comprehension is assessed through questions on the contexts of the reading materials. The main characteristics of this method can be summed up as follows:

(a) The method is divided into intensive and extensive reading. From the beginning, a great amount of reading is undertaken both in and out of class. Pupils are trained to comprehend the meaning directly without translating what they are reading.

(b) Intensive and extensive reading are graded in order to develop gradually the pupil's reading ability.

(c) The vocabulary of the early readings is strictly controlled. Vocabulary, then, is expanded as fast as possible, since the acquisition of vocabulary is considered more important than grammatical skills.

(d) The teaching of grammar rules is based principally on the structures found in the reading passages. Only the grammar necessary for reading is taught.

(e) Minimal attention is paid to pronunciation, whereas translation receives due care.

(f) Writing is restricted to the exercises which might help pupils understand the vocabulary and structures that are necessary to follow the text.

Consequently, the Reading method places a great emphasis on one skill i.e. reading, whereas other skills are neglected. However, this method may be of great benefit for competent learners in that it arouses their curiosity to know about foreign cultures and also increases their ability to read in the foreign language. The Reading method continued to be used till new approaches, namely the structural and later the communicative emerged.

2.4

The Aural-Oral Approach (The Audio-Lingual Method)

Introduction

The last four decades have witnessed a rapid increase in international communication. Many people, across the world, have begun to develop an interest in modern languages. But there was a feeling of discontent with the traditional methods, i.e. the grammar–translation, the Direct and the Reading methods. Many questions were raised about their validity and adequacy especially in their treatment of spoken language. Linguists and teachers became impatient with the ineffective teaching in these methods. Concurrently, research and knowledge in the linguistic sciences as well as experimentation in educational technology and psychology were developing. These movements eventually gave rise to the aural-oral approach which was a reaction to the grammar–translation method and a modification of the Direct method.

The theory implies the acquisition of oral language skills through oral practice based on repetition and learning by analogy. The approach is often referred to as the audio-lingual method.

This method aims at 'developing listening and speaking skills first, as the foundation on which to build the skills of reading and writing' (Rivers 1971, pp. 23–4). In other words, the foreign-language pupil is brought to proficiency in oral and aural use of structures before being taught how to read and write them. The advocates of this method claim that language is essentially acquired through habits and that responses must be drilled until they become automatic and natural. This process reflects a behaviourist view of language learning influenced by the psychologist Skinner. The approach proposed this mechanical process of habit formation through which the phases of stimulus, response and reinforcement would determine the formulation of structure drills and would lead the pupil to the acquisition of these structures.

William Moulton, in 1961, summed up the assumptions on which this method is based as follows:

(a) Language is speech, not writing. That is, it is the spoken aspect of language that concerns structural linguists.

(b) Language is a set of habits. This principle means that language is acquired by imitation and practice. Habits are established by stimulus, response and reinforcement.

(c) Teach the language, not about the language. This means that we must teach pupils 'a set of habits', not a set of rules, as the main goal of language learning is to enable pupils to talk in the language and not to talk about it.

(d) A language is what its native speakers say, not what someone thinks they ought to say. This slogan is a strong reaction against prescriptive traditional grammarians who were concerned to make rules about how people ought to speak and write in accordance with some imposed standard. We should deal with language as it is and not prescribe what other people say.

(e) Languages are different. Languages differ from each other in their sounds and structures. Each language is systematic and sufficient to serve the purpose of the community which speaks it. There is no such a thing as a primitive language.

Implications for teaching

(a) This method gives priority to the spoken language which the pupil needs as an instrument of communication; so it emphasizes listening and speaking and considers them more important than reading and writing. Accordingly, teaching the foreign language should follow the order of listening, speaking, reading and writing. Language teaching courses should reflect this sequence and should teach the language of daily usage.

(b) There is an extended pre-reading period at the beginning of learning the foreign language.

(c) Great importance is attached to pronunciation with special attention to intonation. This objective is realized by intensive pattern practice, much use of tapes and language laboratory, and by the memorization of dialogues regardless of the lexical meaning which is unimportant beside perfect pronunciation.

(d) There is a great effort to prevent pupils' errors and successful responses are immediately reinforced. However, there is a tendency to manipulate language and disregard meaning. Sometimes, especially at the beginning, learners repeat incomprehensible material to make the production of speech automatic and habitual.

(e) The method presents language units in terms of sentence patterns. New material is usually presented orally in pattern drills or dialogue form or with actions or pictures. Dialogues and sentence-pattern drills form the activity of every language lesson. Moreover, dialogues are used as one way of creating situations: buying tickets at the cinema, mailing a letter, booking a room in a hotel, etc. A great deal of language activity is expected from the pupils themselves.

(f) Structures are sequenced and taught one at a time. Structuralists break language into lists of structures and present them in a 'learning order'. Each structural item should be taught before the next item is introduced. Drilling techniques are designed to get rid of errors.

(g) There is little or no grammatical explanation. Rules of grammar are taught by inductive analogy rather than by deductive explanation. Structures are sequenced and taught one at a time. Structural patterns are taught by using pattern practice. The drills of pattern practice require the learner to transform, substitute, replace, expand, integrate, etc.

(h) Vocabulary is strictly limited and learned in appropriate context.

(i) A little use of the mother tongue by the teacher is permitted. Translation is avoided.

The criticisms of the approach can be classified as follows:

(a) This method emphasizes speech at the expense of other language skills, especially writing.

(b) The ordering of listening, speaking, reading and writing is not essential. There is no basic reason why all language skills cannot be taught simultaneously.

(c) The method takes no account of the creative use of language and cognition, as it emphasizes mechanical repetition through the use of oral drills. Empirical evidence, however, has shown that pattern practice, though useful for the early stages of foreign language learning, is not conducive to real communication.

(d) In focusing on the form rather than on the content or meaning, the method fails to prepare the learner to use the foreign language for meaningful communication.

(e) The method equates the acquisition of the rules of the target language with the ability to communicate effectively in it. This is a fallacy. Learning to produce grammatical sentences does not guarantee that one will be able to communicate in situations which require the creative use of speech acts or notions. These include requesting, disagreeing, expressing opinions, showing feelings of sympathy, happiness, or anger, etc.

(f) Finally, this method requires, among other things, small classes, carefully prepared materials and a lot of time. Above all it requires a well-trained teacher who knows 'what to teach' and 'how to teach' adequately. The ineffective application of the technique will produce boredom and fatigue on the part of the learners.

Despite the foregoing limitations, the audio-lingual method is still the most widespread method of foreign language teaching today. The method was adopted in the educational systems of the Arab world in the sixties and continued to be used over the last two decades until it was replaced, in some Arab countries, by the communicative approach.

Nevertheless, the majority of Arab countries are still committed to the aural-oral approach (audio-lingual method). However some modifications have been introduced to make foreign language teaching and learning more interesting and more appropriate. Among these major modifications are situational and contextual teaching.

2.5

Situational and Contextual Teaching

Situational teaching requires the use of physical demonstration of notions and objects in order to present and practise the structures of the language. Actions are simulated to illustrate the utterances, numerous pictures and other real objects are used. Contextual teaching on the other hand attempts to teach the structures of the language in everyday situations where they are likely to occur. These situations are presented in the form of dialogues with titles such as 'at the supermarket', 'going to the post office', 'visiting a friend' or 'a school library', etc. Though contextualization is a vital component in foreign-language teaching and learning, it has its own limitations which can be summed up in the following:

(a) Situations are not graded. They are usually selected at random to serve the purpose of the structures on which they are based.
(b) Learners are not shown how a structure in a particular situation can be used in another.
(c) The utterances and expressions of one social situation are all related to one type. There is little or no deviation from the beginning until the end of the dialogue. In real-life speech we do not generally adhere to the same vocabulary or expressions. Nevertheless the technique of creating situations in the classroom is crucial for effective use of a functional-notional syllabus as will be seen when reviewing the communicative approach.

2.6

The Communicative Approach

Introduction
This is generally referred to as the functional-notional approach. It emerged in the early 1970s as a result of the work of the Council of Europe experts. The approach was designed primarily to meet the needs of adult learners, tourists or people engaged in academic, cultural, technical or economic activities. However, it can be traced to the work of Chomsky in the 1960s, when he advanced the two notions of 'competence' and 'performance' as a reaction against the prevalent audio-lingual method and its views and language learning. These two concepts were developed later on by Hymes, into a 'communicative competence' which refers to the psychological, cultural and social rules which discipline the use of speech. Such competency, as Hymes (1974, p. 277) remarks, is 'fed by social experience, needs and motives, and issues in action that is itself a renewed source of motives, needs and experience'.

This new concept of 'communicative competence' has been expanded by a number of writers including Bung (1973), Trim (1973), Van Ek (1973), Alexander (1976), Wilkins (1976), Stratton (1977), Dobson (1977), Finocchiaro (1979) and Richterich (1980). They have proposed seven categories of communicative functions, which are requesting and giving information, expressing thought processes, expressing opinions, moral discipline and evaluation, modifying people's behaviour, expressing personal feelings and interacting socially. Under each of these categories there are many notions or purposes. Other categories have also been identified to serve the learner's immediate communicative purposes and to facilitate interaction between speakers from the first lesson of learning the foreign language. Nevertheless, such notion lists have not been universally adopted as a compact syllabus, on the part of teachers and educators. The stress of the approach on communication and conversation has rapidly gained popularity. The pupil learns from the beginning that language is communication, that it is something to be used. The implication of this is that we are more concerned with what people do with language than with what they know of it. In another sense, this communicative methodology tries to gear language teaching to the rules we need for communicating appropriately in social situations rather than to the grammatical rules we need for producing correct sentences.

Principles and Characteristics

The basic principles underlying the communicative approach are as follows:

(a) The theory of language learning underlying the approach is holistic rather than behaviouristic. It assumes that 'language acquisition depends not only on exposure to environmental stimulation but also on specific innate propensities of the organism' (Hwang 1970).

   Thus, language acquisition is seen as a creative process, not as habit formation. The idea of language learning by a stimulus–response process is rejected.

(b) Communicative competence, as spelt out by Widdowson (1984), implies knowledge of the grammatical system of the language as well as performance. In other words such competence includes both the usage and the use of the language. Hence the approach does not deny the importance of mastering grammatical forms, so long as they are taught as a means of carrying out meaningful communication. That is, grammar is taught as the intuitive knowledge of language use – a language tool rather than a language aim.

(c) Unlike the audio-lingual method, the communicative approach gives priority to the semantic content of language learning. That is, pupils learn the grammatical form through meaning, and not the other way round. This new strategy helps the learners apply what they have learnt of the linguistic knowledge, without any difficulty, to real life situations involving interactive processes.

(d) One aspect of communication is the interaction between speakers. This approach provides communicative functions (uses) and notions (semantic themes and language items). These functions reflect more closely real life use of the language as they are usually connected with real situations, and with pupils' needs and interests. Naturally, in more realistic settings, the communicative act will be intrinsically motivating. Moreover, pupils learn to manipulate language varieties that differ according to the degree of formality or informality of the situation, the topic or activity undertaken, and the mode of the discourse, whether oral or written. In other words, they must recognize register when communicating with others – which language variety is appropriate with different people in different situations – for example, employer–employee, teacher–pupil, pupil–pupil, doctor–patient, parent–child, etc.

(e) Related to the above point is the fact that the approach, along with sociolinguistic considerations, sets out to incorporate sociocultural allusions and psycholinguistic components. These factors give learners motives, facts and basic cultural insights for immediate use in realistic situations. They also induce them to use the target language in learning something, doing something and contributing something of themselves.

(f) The approach sets realistic learning tasks and activities that create situations in which, for example,

> questions must be asked, information recorded, information recovered from text, knowledge, ideas, reminiscences exchanged, emotions and attitudes expressed in one way or another, in which the student has the opportunity to experience participant and observer language roles, and in which language skills must be used (i) to make sense of information, experience, ideas and feelings for oneself, and (ii) to solve problems, discuss, consult, instruct, share, argue, organize (Levine 1972).

Such procedures and techniques will help pupils, who become the centre of the learning process, to develop their communicative competence as they provide them with the potential ability and motivation to discover the answers for themselves in groups, pairs or individually. However, this strategy requires the teacher to relinquish his or her role as a model to be imitated or the giver of knowledge. He or she must be seen as the guide or manager of the class, encouraging the pupils to communicate their real thoughts and ideas.

(g) Since the primary aim of the approach is to prepare learners for meaningful communication, errors are tolerated. Pupils are encouraged to risk error in communicating information or their thoughts and feelings. Fluency is given more weight than accuracy, so language teachers must not insist upon mastery of the material when it is first presented. Linguistic items and functions and notions are recycled in a logical sequence during the course and they can be studied in greater depth as pupils progress in their study.

(h) The communicative methodology does not assume that the teacher is the centre of all classroom activities. He or she is no longer the prime mover, or the instructor with the pupils acting as listeners or respondents. Instead, the focus is shifted to the pupils and their interests, abilities and everyday life concerns. In other words, the communicative methodology is a pupil-centred approach to foreign language learning. Learners are not only recipients or respondents but also active participants. The teacher's role is that of an organizer of activities.

Pedagogical Implications

(a) There is emphasis on communication, that is, the ability to use the language, from the very beginning. The main objective is to enable pupils to use the language to express their needs.

(b) The classroom atmosphere tends to be relaxed so that pupils can enjoy their English lessons.

(c) Group work, individual instruction and co-operative work are encouraged.

(d) Pupils are given the chance to initiate questions and express their opinions.

(e) The lesson procedure is based on activities through which new language items are presented and practised.

(f) Teachers assist pupils in any way that motivates them to learn the language and to work with it.

(g) The centre of classroom activities is transferred from the teacher to the pupil and this leads to socialization.

(h) A highly competent and imaginative teacher is a major requirement for the successful application of the method.

(i) Comprehensive preparation on the part of the teacher is required.

(j) Grammatical forms are approached through meaning. Pupils, when learning a new item of grammar, must acquire two of its aspects: the grammatical form and the meaning underlying it. Deductive explanation of grammar is preferred.

(k) The importance of comprehension is emphasized, especially listening comprehension.

(l) Pronunciation is not emphasized. However, comprehensible pronunciation is desirable.

(m) The language skills – both written and spoken – are equally emphasized. They can start from the first day of learning the foreign language.

(n) Errors are considered inevitable in the process of language learning. The teacher need not correct every mistake of the pupil's language as this will inhibit him and prevent him from developing his communicative competence. Regular practice, remedial work and interpretation can improve pupils' English.

(o) Repetition (i.e. repetitive drills, or dialogues) is discouraged.

(p) The use of teaching media especially audio-visual aids is essential.

(q) Learning activities are also important in order to contextualize the teaching points. Situations, dialogues, improvisation, role-playing, problem-solving, interviews, debates, games, and the like are necessary to give the pupils a chance to practise the language.

(r) There is a renewed interest in the teaching of lexis to improve communicative competence. Pupils are required to learn a wide range of conventional and idiomatic expressions in addition to the expansion of passive vocabulary for reading purposes.

(s) A closer link is required between the classroom activities and their transfer to the real world outside.

(t) Using the mother tongue is permitted to save time and effort when explaining difficult items.

(u) The teachers' and pupils' motivation and positive attitude are crucial for effective teaching and learning.

Shortcomings of the Approach

In spite of the merits which characterize the communicative approach, it has been subjected to many criticisms, some of which were summed up as follows (See Swan, 1985):

(a) The approach relies extensively on the functional-notional syllabus which places heavy demands on the pupils. This is especially true at the initial stages of learning because of their lack of speaking rules and cultural insights.

(b) The various categories of language functions are overlapping and not systematically graded like the structures of the language. This creates some confusion and makes it difficult to teach the functions properly.

(c) One of the major tenets of the communicative approach is 'the rules of use or rules of communication'. They determine the understanding or interpretation of various utterances. However, there has been no precise definition of what form such rules might take. This is left to the discretion of the teacher. Utterances acquire their communicative value from the context or the situation they are used in, not from the supposed rules of communication. In this connection, Swan (1985, p. 50) remarks that rules of use 'are non-language specific and that the precise value of an utterance is given by the interaction of its structural and lexical meaning with the situation in which it is used'.

(d) This approach assumes that one can learn a foreign language best through appropriate exposure to communicative acts (i.e. functions) in speech discourse such as role-playing, dialogues and interviews. However, empirical evidence has shown that this concept is idealistic rather than realistic since it is possible, as Wilkins points out, that 'a learner who already has an advanced knowledge of the lexical and grammatical systems of a language can himself go a long way towards inferring the communicative functions of utterances to which the systems are applied' (Wilkins 1972, p. 14).

From a practical point of view, effective teaching involves, notional, functional, situational, phonological, lexical and structural skills along with some practice of repetition, rote learning, grammar explanation, translation and structural drilling. It is thus quite possible for a text-book based on a structural syllabus to be highly communicative.

(e) A major premise underlying the communicative approach is its emphasis on pupils' needs and interests. This implies that every teacher should modify the syllabus to correspond with the needs of his pupils. This is not possible to implement as it will require the teacher to write a separate syllabus for each pupil in the class. Such a goal is very ambitious and impossible to realize.

(f) The concept of appropriateness in this approach is over-valued as there is much focusing on the meaning of speech acts and utterances.[1] No one would deny that appropriateness is a requirement for fluent communication. But in this approach it has a unique dimension which leads one to believe that the secret of successful language teaching lies in incorporating appropriateness into every speech act or item. Appropriateness is not, however, new to language learning or an innovation of the communicative approach. It was employed by other approaches as well. It was known as the 'register' or variation of language; namely, formal, informal, familiar, conventional, idiomatic, taboo, colloquial and jargon. The problem with appropriateness is that though the approach stresses it as an essential aspect of communicative competence, it is neglected in communicative testing, especially oral competence.

(g) A basic communicative principle is that previous approaches to foreign language teaching did not give real or proper concern to meaning. As a reaction to this claimed limitation, the communicative approach gives priority to meanings and rules of use rather than to grammar and rules of structure. The latter, according to the communicative theory, are taught by means of functions and notions. Such concentration on language behaviour may result in negative consequences. Thus the pupils may not have sufficient knowledge of grammar to do things with the language, i.e. to perform communicative tasks. There is also the danger of not covering all areas of grammar when they are solely taught through functions and notions. This shortcoming may lead pupils to overgeneralize as they may believe that one particular form can only express a specific function. Moreover, the teacher may not be able to isolate and practise difficult forms of grammar before pupils can utilize them in speech acts. In this respect Swan (1985, p. 50) remarks that 'it is no use making meaning tidy if grammar then becomes so untidy that it cannot be learnt properly'.

(h) Communicative testing is neither valid nor reliable and the entire process is confusing. For it is still not clear how one can measure language appropriateness in the context of actual communication.

(i) There are two major requirements for the successful application of the approach. One is the availability of a classroom that can allow for group work activities or for pupil–pupil interaction and for teaching aids and materials. Such a classroom is desirable but unfortunately is not available in most schools. The other requirement is a highly competent and imaginative teacher who is able to apply the audio-lingual techniques appropriately. Ineffective application of the techniques is detrimental and might discourage pupils from learning the language. In the Arab world such teachers are scarce. Consequently, we cannot expect adequate application of the communicative methodology.

---

[1] Appropriateness in this context indicates the proper use of words; notions, utterances and gestures in relation to setting and people involved in the communicative interaction. Has the speaker used suitable words and ideas and delivered them appropriately?

However, despite these limitations and demerits, the communicative approach has contributed many ideas and strategies to foreign language methodology. It has helped in the analysis of teaching the language of interaction, brought into focus the communicative purpose of language learning, and shifted attention to pupils' needs and interests. Above all, it has transformed the traditional role of the teacher as the sole giver of knowledge to that of a receiver of information, from the dominant figure in the classroom to that of a manager and co-ordinator of the class.

The approach, though still evolving, has gained increased popularity in many educational systems across the world. Many Arab countries especially those of the Gulf States have recently adopted a modified version of the approach to teaching English with the aim of improving the communicative competence of the pupils.

2.7

The Eclectic Approach

In spite of the proliferation of theories of language-teaching, no language teacher applies exclusively any of the given or known teaching theories. Teachers often incorporate features of different approaches in their particular methodology. Thus their teaching may be based on the communicative theory, but supplemented with a careful grading of words and grammatical forms and structures so that the pupils can develop gradually and simultaneously both their communicative competence and knowledge of the language system. The use of many different practical approaches is very common among foreign language teachers. They feel that such practices overcome the problems associated with theoretical approaches, and increase their professional competence.

The eclectic approach is, therefore, a framework involving procedures and techniques drawn from various methods. It is useful in practical situations in the classroom. It is not based on a specific theory or discipline; but there are some assumptions underlying it. These can be summed up as follows:

(a) Each one of the well-known methods (e.g. grammar–translation, reading, audio-lingual and communicative) has its own features. This is significant because there is no one method which is comprehensive enough to meet the requirements of effective teaching and learning, or to cater for the problems of FL teachers in classroom application. It is true that some teaching methods are better or more effective than others. Yet they all have some weaknesses and some strengths. Experienced teachers are very sensitive to the limitations of different methods, so they reject the weak points of each approach and retain only those aspects that are applicable in the particular teaching situation in which they find themselves.

(b) The frequent shifts of methodology have made teachers feel that it is better to have a combination of elements from all of them. Methods may supplement one another especially when there is no one method which can fulfil all language goals and programme objectives.

A major premise of eclecticism is that the teaching process should serve the pupils, not a particular method. Hence teachers should feel free to choose the techniques or procedures that best fit the pupils' needs and the teaching–learning situation.

Chapter Three

Factors Influencing Methods

Introduction

The preceding chapter has shown that there is no single method that can accommodate all the requirements of foreign language teachers. The reason for this shortcoming is that the process of teaching and learning involves other factors which have to be taken into consideration in each methodology. They are the *teacher, the pupil, objectives of instruction, psychology of learning, learning activities, time available, classroom situation* and *motivation*. Each of these factors is discussed in subsequent sections. It may be added that other variables such as the nature of the foreign language, attitudes towards learning it, and the social context are important in determining a methodology. However, they are not discussed here because of their diversity. The importance of motivation will be discussed in Chapter 17. The others are considered in this chapter.

3.1

The FL Teacher

The teacher is instrumental in creating the conditions for learning. His competence is reflected in his understanding of the nature of foreign language teaching and learning, his knowledge of teaching theories and methods and his expertise in communicative practice. Methods and objectives of instruction are determined by the teacher's professional skill. Thus, a teacher who has difficulty in speaking English will not succeed in giving his pupils a good command of spoken language or be able to teach communicatively. Similarly, if he is not a master in role-playing techniques, all his teaching will be 'chalk and talk' to the disadvantage of his pupils. Furthermore, if he is not familiar with the principles and details of the method used, he will not be able to employ it effectively.

Since the teacher's role is so crucial, the question arises as to what is required of a competent foreign language teacher. In theory, an English language teacher should be one who

(a) has a practical command of English skills – speaking, understanding, reading and writing;
(b) has a sound knowledge of the English sound system, grammar and lexis;
(c) is a master of communicative techniques, functions and notions;
(d) is a drill master;
(e) is a motivator;
(f) is an evaluator;
(g) has a knowledge of applied linguistics;
(h) is trained in psycholinguistics as well as sociolinguistics;
(i) has a good knowledge of English culture or literature;
(j) is interested in the job and is professionally well-informed;
(k) has personal charm, patience, a sense of humour and a talent for discipline;
(l) has a friendly attitude towards the language, pupils and colleagues.
(See Altas, 1981.)

3.2
The Pupil

When preparing his teaching materials or lessons, the teacher should take into account the pupils' age, intrinsic motivation, attitude, ability, previous language experience and native language and attitude to the target language. These factors are important in the learning process; and the teacher will have to stimulate learning through varied appeals and methods. For example, while games and play activities may be effective with young learners, older pupils would prefer more adult learning activities such as role playing, drama and classroom discussion.

Because learning English is often compulsory in schools, the problem of motivation turns into the problem of creating the desire among pupils to learn English. Lack of motivation (i.e. external motives) might turn into a hostile attitude towards the foreign language and the FL teacher.

Another important factor is the pupils' mother tongue which might influence the learning process adversely, especially when there are no similarities between it and the target language. Arabic and English are good examples of this as the two languages are not cognates. They differ in sound, structure, vocabulary and writing systems. In such a situation, the teacher has to indicate the major points of difficulty. He must also be aware of the probable areas of interference so as to plan techniques and materials for helping pupils to overcome them.

3.3
Objectives of Instruction

The basis of a sound method of foreign language teaching is knowing what the objectives of teaching are as these determine the desired goals of learning. The teacher should have a clear idea of the syllabus aims so as to be able to decide what kinds of language skills will be of greater value to the learners. This in turn will enable him to choose his materials and techniques appropriately.

However, setting up attainable objectives requires consideration of a number of pertinent factors. These include the skill of the teacher, the size of the class, the time available for the course; the number of hours a day for English classes, availability of teaching materials, facilities, and the like. It would be unrealistic to expect a teacher to set objectives which he himself is not capable of reaching. For instance, to try to get pupils to master the spoken language when the teacher's own oral fluency leaves much to be desired is a difficult task. Similarly, the amount of time allotted for instruction determines the objectives we desire to achieve.

The number of pupils in the class is also a significant factor in determining the type of objectives desired. For example, oral proficiency is difficult to achieve in classes of more than, say, thirty pupils because the teacher will be unable to employ techniques for oral practice with such numbers.

3.4
Psychology of Learning

It is still difficult to determine the contribution of the psychology of learning to foreign language acquisition, since the principles vary according to the theory or method used. Thus the audio-lingual method views language learning as habit formation. On the other hand, the communicative approach views language learning as an interactive and cognitive process. However, there are some psychological factors which have a direct and indirect effect on the learning process and consequently the methodology of teaching. Among these are the following:

(a) Learning is effective when the teaching materials and activities are related to the pupils' needs and experiences.
(b) Both integrative and instrumental motivation are of primary importance in learning.
(c) Gradation and logical sequence of the teaching materials, e.g. language functions, notions and activities, within larger grammatical categories, facilitate the implementation of the method adopted and the learning process as well.
(d) Learning is enhanced when pupils can perceive meaningful association between teaching materials and real life situations. The stronger the relation, the greater the likelihood of retention and more immediate the recall.
(e) The same language item (a structure or a function) should be reintroduced in many situations to gain reinforcement and better learning on the part of the pupils.
(f) Since the pupil restructures what he is taught, he must become an active participant in the learning process.
(g) Repetition and reinforcement are needed, now and then, to develop fluency in English. Incorrect responses should be eliminated as quickly as possible. However, correction must not inhibit pupils from further participation, or prevent them from developing confidence.
(h) Group work, pair work and classroom activities in general should be determined by the pupils' ability and different rates of learning.
(i) Illustration of language items is necessary. The teacher should help his pupils, through various means, to perceive the relationships between the elements of the language.
(j) Transfer of learning occurs properly only when pupils are given enough examples, linguistic/functional drills and learning tasks.

3.5
Learning Activities

When the learning objectives are established, it is essential to assign the linguistic, functional and learning activities that can best fulfil the specified FL objectives. Thus, if the goal is to develop a reasonable oral communicative competence, pupils should be provided with activities that are conducive to oral communication. If, on the other hand, the aim is to enable pupils to read and write the language adequately, most of the teaching should focus on reading and writing activities. The procedures and techniques which lead to oral fluency differ greatly from those designed to teach reading and writing. The quantity and quality of each technique or activity in the classroom should reflect its place in the overall objectives. However, if the four language skills, namely, speaking, understanding speech, reading and writing constitute the main objectives of English language teaching, a proper balance of learning activities must be established. Consequently, there is no reason to over-emphasize one type of activity at the expense of others.

3.6
Time Available

The time devoted to FL teaching and learning is of paramount importance. The success of attaining FL objectives depends largely on the hours allocated to language teaching.

Some techniques and teaching strategies require more time than others, and if the teacher wants to cater for the individual problems of his pupils, he will need more time than prescribed in order to work in different ways with different pupils. But the time frame is fixed. In fact, in some Arab educational systems, the FL hours have recently been reduced to the minimum five hours per week. This time is inadequate and results in improper implementation of any methodology to be used. It also leads to ineffective teaching or learning. In such conditions, unless the teacher provides for individualized instruction the whole English programme will be liable to failure.

3.7
The Classroom Situation

A classroom should be attractive, comfortable, well-ventilated, well-equipped with teaching aids and materials, and large enough to allow group work or role play activities. Besides, the size of the class should be normal (about thirty pupils in each room) in order to ensure more active pupil participation in learning especially when the main objective of English instruction is the mastery of oral fluency. In large classes, oral interaction is limited to one exchange at a time, whether teacher–pupil or pupil–pupil. Large classes also make it difficult for the teacher to supervise every pupil which means ineffective teaching and learning.

Part Three

Teaching Language Elements

Chapter Four

Teaching Pronunciation

Introduction

The teaching of pronunciation is an important aspect of foreign language methodology.[1] Pronunciation drills are an integral part of effective English language teaching. These drills help pupils overcome problems that arise from the interference of the mother tongue. Thus, when an Arab child is first introduced to English at the age of ten, he will have acquired the phonological system of Arabic. If he has no remedial work on pronunciation at an early stage of learning the foreign language, he will establish incorrect forms of English sounds. Features and habits of the mother tongue will condition the way he pronounces English. It is essential, therefore, to start teaching the sounds and intonational patterns of English from the first day of learning the language. This procedure will foster good habits of pronunciation in young learners. Practice in the early stages of learning should be, however, limited to minimal pairs[2] or to the repetition of individual words or patterns.

With advanced learners, pronunciation practice may be done within the context of more difficult drills. For example, learners should be exposed to living speech (live or recorded), such as conversations, radio broadcasts, plays, and the like. Such pronunciation drills and activities will help pupils indentify and discriminate English sounds. They also enable them to hear English voices other than the teacher's, and they provide the pupils with a model for imitation.

However, the teaching of pronunciation which involves individual sounds, liaison between these sounds, stress, rhythm and intonation, may run into problems. These include the availability of a competent teacher, authentic materials, adequate exposure to good models and constant practising.

---

[1] The norm of pronunciation used here is the RP model which is internationally intelligible.
[2] A minimal pair is two words which are pronounced alike except for one sound only, e.g.: fill/fell, pen/ten, lip/tip. This difference results in a semantic difference. It is these contrasting sounds of each pair that we want the pupils to listen to and repeat.

The teacher must have a basic understanding of how the sound system of English works. Moreover, he should know the problems which may affect the learning process such as the substitution of the phoneme /b/ for /p/ as in /piːpɔl/ which is often pronounced by an Arab learner as /biːbɔl/. This contrastive knowledge will help the teacher to identify problem areas and to handle them more effectively. To fulfil this goal, the teacher has to design learning activities that will elicit pupils' responses, requiring the use of vocabulary items or grammatical structures which contain the target sounds he wishes them to practise. In this way the teacher contextualizes pronunciation practice and ensures meaningful communication, the central purpose of language study.

For pedagogical purposes, we shall review in this chapter (a) segmental phonemes (consonants and vowels), (b) suprasegmentals including stress, intonation and internal juncture, (c) English sounds (including consonant clusters) that do not exist in Arabic, indicating at the same time habits and features of Arabic that might affect English pronunciation, and finally (d) some pronunciation drills and activities are suggested to overcome the influence of the habits of the mother-tongue.

4.1

Consonant Sounds

Phoneme	Example	Description
A. Stops		
p	pin, rip	Voiceless, bilabial[1]
b	bite, rib	Voiced, bilabial
t	tin, night	Voiceless, alveolar
d	day, ride	Voiced, alveolar
k	kin, back	Voiceless, velar
g	gun, bag	Voiced, velar
B. Fricative		
f	five, leaf	Voiceless, labiodental
v	vivid, leave	Voiced, labiodental
θ	thigh, breath	Voiceless, dental
ð	then, bathe	Voiced, dental
s	sun, bus	Voiceless, alveolar
z	zoo, eyes	Voiced, alveolar
Š/ʃ	shine, bush	Voiceless, alveopalatal
Ž/ʒ	rouge, measure	Voiced, alveopalatal
h	hair, hen	Voiceless, glottal
C. Affricates		
Č/tʃ	chair, beach	Voiceless, alveopalatal
J̌/dʒ	jar, judge	Voiced, alveopalatal
D. Nasals		
m	man, drum	Voiced, bilabial
n	nine, knee	Voiced, alveolar
ŋ	sing, rung	Voiced, velar

[1] Voiced sounds are made with the vocal cords vibrating, e.g. /b/, /d/ whereas voiceless sounds are not accompanied with such vibration, e.g. /p/, /t/. All vowels are voiced, e.g. /i/, /o/.

E. *Liquids*

| r | rain, red | Voiced, alveolar |
| l | led, miller | Voiced, alveolar |

F. *Glides*

| w | wet, bow | Voiced, bilabial |
| y | yet, boy | Voiced, alveopalatal |

the voiced consonant phonemes are: /b/, /d/, /g/, /l/, /m/, /n/, /r/, /ð/, /v/, /w/, /j/, /z/, /ʒ/, /dʒ/.

The voiceless consonant phonemes are: /f/, /h/, /k/, /p/, /s/, /ʃ/, /t/, /θ/, /tʃ/.

Pupils can learn voiced and unvoiced consonants by pairing them (the voiced consonant is first): b/p; d/t; g/k; ð/θ; v/f; z/s; ʒ/ʃ, dʒ/tʃ.

The sounds /p/, /ŋ/, /v/, /r/, /t/, /θ/, and /ð/ are very difficult to Arab learners of English. Their difficulty is due to tongue position or to their absence in Arabic.

Arabic lacks the /p/ phoneme; so an Arab learner often confuses it with the voiced bilabial plosive /b/.[1] Thus, he might pronounce /kʌp/ as /kʌb/, /pet/ as /bet/, /prɪns/ as /brɪns/, and so on.

A great problem is posed by the voiced nasal /ŋ/ which an Arab speaker of English always replaces by (ŋg) in medial and final positions. He can be expected to pronounce /sɪŋɪŋ/ as /sɪŋgɪŋ/ /jʌŋ/ as /jʌŋg/ /rɪŋ/ as /rɪŋg/, etc.

English /v/, is sometimes replaced by the voiceless labio-dental /f/, since /v/ does not exist in Arabic. Thus the Arab pupil may pronounce /vjuː/ as /fjuː/, /faiv/ as /faif/, /seven/ as /sefn/, and the like.

A type of /r/ similar to the Scottish one exists in Arabic and is pronounced in all positions, whether followed by a consonant or a vowel sound or coming finally in the word. For instance, an Arab learner of English tends to pronounce /pɑːk/ as /bɑːrk/, /mɑːstə/ as /mɑːstər/ and /gəːl/ as /gəːrl/.

/t/ is alveolar in English but dental in Arabic and is often not aspirated; whereas English /θ/ and /ð/ exist in Arabic as separate phonemes. The problem with them is in the written and not in the spoken form because their orthography is the same. Pupils find it difficult to differentiate /θ/ from /ð/ in such words as think/then; bath/bathe; nothing/weather, etc.

4.2

English and Arabic Clusters

Consonant clusters in Arabic and English differ greatly. English has as many as four element consonant clusters, while Arabic does not permit clusters of more than two consonants. The following table summarizes this difference:

	Initial	Medial	Final
English	C	C	C
	CC	CC	CC
	CCC	CCC	CCC
	—	CCCC	CCCC
Arabic	C	C	C
		CC	CC

This situation causes real problems for an Arab learner of English. However, he does not encounter difficulty in pronouncing two-element clusters because they exist in Arabic as in words like /həbl/ – (rope) /ʃtuul/ – (how long). But

---

[1] A phoneme is the smallest unit of speech that can identify and distinguish words in a language, e.g. in *pay* and *bay* only the sounds /p/ and /b/ make the meaning different.

three consonant sequences do constitute a problem to an Arab learner. Very often, after the mother-tongue patterns, he inserts the vowel /i/ between the first and the last two consonants to break the cluster so as to be able to pronounce it. Thus:

street	/striːt/	becomes	/sitriːt/
spread	/spred/	becomes	/sipred/
spring	/sprɪŋ/	becomes	/sipring/
midst	/mɪdst/	becomes	/midist/

It is clear from the above examples that the problem of pronunciation is solved by the intrusive /i/ phoneme.

Another feature of this breaking of consonant clusters is observed when pronouncing the past tense of regular verbs such as: looked, stopped, touched, etc. this is a result of spelling deciding pronunciation because Arabic is a phonetic language.

Mistakes with consonant clusters are more common than those with single consonants. Special exercises should be given in order to practise producing the clusters which are not found in Arabic.

4.3.
Gemination

Next to the problem of clusters is gemination which is characteristic of Arabic. We mean by gemination, here, the lengthening of the same consonant (or vowel). This problem is common with words containing double letters such as connect, collect, correct, etc. Arab learners interpret them as phonemic length which is not the case, so they pronounce them as /konnekt/, /kollekt/ and /kərrekt/.

4.4
English and Arabic Vowels

English and Arabic have two different vowel structures. There are nine simple vowels and five glides (i.e. diphthongs) in English: /iː/, /ɪ/, /e/, /æ/, /ʌ/, /ɑː/, /uː/, /ʊ/, /ɔ/, /ɪə/, /eɪ/, /aɪ/, /aʊ/, /ɔɪ/ and /əʊ/. Arabic, on the other hand, has six vowels and three glides. The Arabic vowel system consists of three pairs of vowels. The vowels in each pair are distinguished by length. The long/short pairs and the glides are as follows:

a –	/ā/ as in /bāb/	door
	/a/ as in /rab/	the Lord
b –	/ī/ as in /fīl/	elephant
	/i/ as in /min/	from
c –	/ū/ as in /nūr/	light
	/u/ as in /kul/	all
1 –	/ay/ as in /kay/	in order to
2 –	/āy/ as in /ʃāy/	tea
3 –	/aw/ as in /aw/	or

The English vowel system is relatively complex. Vowels are usually described by the position of the tongue, whether it is relatively high, mid, or low; front, back or central; and by the shape of the lips, whether rounded or stretched. The vowel variations, for example, in words like bite, bit, bait, bet, pot, bat, bought, boat, put, but, boot and bout can be difficult for an Arab learner to discriminate in listening, speaking and reading.

Apart from the fact that an Arab learner has a poor mastery of English vowels, there is still the problem of the length of the vowels /aɪ/, /iː/, /ɔː/ and /uː/. An Arab learner often pronounces these vowels as the short vowels /a/, /i/, /ɔ/ and /ʊ/ respectively. Thus, instead of saying /grɑːs/ and /bɑːθ/, he would say /græs/ and /bæθ/.

The phonemes /iː/, /ɔː/, and /uː/ are pronounced considerably longer in English than in Arabic. The Arab learner, under the influence of the mother tongue, often transfers the quantity of the Arabic vowel to its English equivalent. Thus he often pronounces:

/pəliːs/ ·	as	/bɔlɪs/	police
/tɔːk/	as	/tɔk/	talk
/duː/	as	/du/	do etc.

Because of their high frequency and different structure, English vowels constitute one of the difficult problems in mastering the sound system of English.

Of the eight English diphthongs, six constitute a problem to an Arab learner of English. These are: /eɪ/, /əʊ/, /ɪə/, /ɪə/, /eə/, and /ʊə/. They are often mispronounced owing to interference from the mother tongue.

The diphthong /eɪ/ is often replaced by the pure long vowel /eː/ found in colloquial Arabic. Thus /reɪn/, /greɪt/ and /feɪl/ are pronounced by Arab pupils as /reːn/, /greːt/ and /feːl/.

The diphthong /əʊ/ is often replaced by the pure vowel /ɔː/. For example /gəʊl/, /bəʊt/ and /kəʊt/ are often pronounced by Arab learners as /gɔːl/, /bɔːt/ and /kɔːt/.

As for the contouring diphthongs /ɪə/, /eə/, /ɔɪ/ and /ʊə/, they are often replaced by the pure vowels /iː/, /eː/, /ɔː/ and /uː/, for example:

/tuːr/	for	tour
/juːr/	for	your
/puːr/	for	poor
/ɪndʒuːr/	for	endure, etc.

In the above examples, the silent (r) is usually pronounced by Arab pupils owing to the influence of Arabic, which is a more phonetically spelt language than English.

4.5
Suprasegmental Features

Suprasegmentals include stress and rhythm, juncture (pause) and intonation. These features, however, are artificial distinctions, made only in order to study the spoken language. They are usually present in any utterance, and the native speaker is quite unconscious of them. Since they are phonemic i.e. they produce differences in meaning, an Arab learner finds some difficulty in mastering them or even in producing proper English utterances. Because of their vital role in understanding or uttering spoken English adequately and intelligibly, each of them is defined below.

4.6
Stress and Rhythm

Stress is the relative degree of loudness of a syllable or a word, or of a syllable within an utterance. These are usually called *word stress* and *sentence stress*. Word stress is often called *accent*.

There are four levels of stress in English namely,
1. Primary, or loudest, stress, usually marked   /

2. Secondary, or second loudest, stress, usually marked   \\
3. Tertiary, or third loudest, stress, usually marked   ∧
4. Weak, or the least loud, stress, usually marked   ∨

Word Stress

Word stress can be phonemic. A good example of this is the word *record*. As a noun, the word is accented on the first syllable. Here the noun RECord is pronounced /rekord/. As a verb the word is stressed on the second syllable. For example: You should record the minutes of the meeting. Here, the verb reCORD is pronounced /rikoːrd/.[1]

Two- or more-syllabled words have their own stress systems, as follows:

1. Two-syllabled words are stressed mostly on the first syllable, e.g.: 'broken, 'handsome, 'curtain, 'picture, 'farmer, 'baby, etc.[2]

2. Two-syllabled words beginning with a prefix of some kind (a-, per-, dis-, re-, com-, ex-, ab-, etc.) are usually stressed on the second syllable. Examples: a'way, be'hind, per'sist, dis'miss, re'ply, com'mit, ex'ceed, etc.

3. Some three-syllabled words have their stress on the middle syllable. Examples: im'portant, re'ceiver, ap'proval, con'dition, de'velop, etc.

4. Some other three-syllabled words are stressed on the first syllable. Examples: 'wonderful, 'absolute, 'ignorant, 'covering, 'hopefully, etc.

5. Four- or more-syllabled words have often two stresses – secondary and primary on the third syllable from the end, e.g., ˌeco'nomic, ˌpo'tential, ˌinor'ganic.

6. Combinations are treated as one word and usually have their stress on the first part. Examples: 'dining room, 'handbag, 'notebook, 'inkpot, 'bookcase, 'classroom, 'football, etc.

7. Nouns modified by other words have their own normal stress patterns, as in the following groups: a 'stone 'building, a 'cotton 'shirt, a 'wooden 'door, a 'green 'bag, an 'old 'house.

8. Words that function as both nouns and verbs have the stress on the first syllable when they are nouns, and on the second syllable when they function as verbs. Examples: contrast, extract, increase, protest, progress, record, insult, export and import.

The above categories of word stress are by no means exhaustive. Many English words have to be learned through imitation and practice because their stress distribution is irregular. The teacher should thus expose his pupils to authentic speech as spoken by its native speakers, and should speak at a normal speed to encourage them to follow his example. Taped material is helpful in this respect, especially if it is practised in the language laboratory.

In Arabic, the stress falls on the last syllable of a word containing two long (or short and long) syllables. This stress habit often causes problems to the Arab learner of English as it is usually retained, thereby affecting the

---

[1] In the above examples, the silent(r) is usually pronounced by Arab students under the influence of Arabic which is a phonetically spelt language.

[2] A mark ' is placed in front of the syllable that is to be stressed. The sign ˌ shows a secondary stress.

acquisition of the new sound system. This difficulty is obvious with two-syllable words (such as subject, record, rebel, project, conduct, etc.) that may be used as either nouns or verbs, with a difference in stress to indicate the difference in meaning. In the absence of such a process in Arabic, pupils often confuse these two-syllable words.

A combination of two nouns also constitutes a problem to an Arab learner because a shift in the primary or the secondary stress makes a difference in meaning. Examples:

a gréenhòuse = a glassed enclosure for cultivating plants.
a grêen house = a house that is green in colour.
an Énglish tèacher = a teacher of the English language.
an Ênglish téacher = a teacher who is from England.

Because the stress pattern is unmarked in writing, the context will be sufficient to clarify the meaning.

Sentence Stress

English sentence stress is not fixed and this causes problems to Arab learners. Each sentence has its own stress pattern. Stress may occur on any word in the utterance depending on what we want to convey. Consider the sentence 'Where did she go yesterday?' The stress may be on 'she' with focus on the person, or on 'where' to show emphasis on the place, or on 'yesterday' to stress the time. Another example of contrastive stress is 'She ate three eggs in the morning'. Thus the speaker may stress the word 'she' to mean that it was she and not he who did the eating; or he may stress the word 'three' to mean that she ate three and not one or two; he also may focus on the word 'morning' to show that the action, i.e. the eating, took place in the morning and not in the afternoon.

As a general rule, the words that are stressed, in a normal sentence are adverbs, adjectives, main verbs or nouns. In contrast, articles, auxiliary verbs, pronouns, prepositions and conjunctions receive tertiary or weak stresses. However, the emphatic 'do' takes a primary stress.

As in word stress, the teacher is requested to expose his pupils to authentic English as spoken by native speakers, and to encourage them to repeat after a model. Pupils learn stressed syllables most effectively by hearing and repeating complete utterances properly spoken.

4.7

Internal Juncture

This refers to the pause between the combination of two nouns characterized by a secondary–primary stress pattern. In other words, the lighter stress falls on the first syllable and the stronger one on the second element, i.e. component. For instance, white house (a house that is white in colour), black + bird, ice + cream, etc. This feature of the English sound system is phonemic. The teacher should be aware of it as the exchange of this stress pattern (i.e. secondary–primary) will change the meaning of the combination. Consider the combination 'blackboard'. When the stress falls on the first part 'black', the word does not mean 'a board that is black in colour', but 'a smooth board (green or black) used especially in schools for writing or drawing'. Notice also the difference in meaning between ice-cream and 'I scream'.

4.8

Intonation

Intonation is the name given to the rising and falling of the voice as we speak or to the levels of pitch in a sentence.[1]

Intonation is phonemic, as any change in the intonation pattern of the sentence will add meaning or implication to the basic meaning of the sentence. A knowledge of its use is, therefore, of primary importance in foreign language learning in order to avoid incorrect interpretation of the speaker's attitudes or feelings.

Intonation is related to sentence stress, since the accented syllable is often spoken on the highest note. There are two important intonation patterns in English:

1. *Pattern 231* (rising-falling intonation) is used

   (a) Simple statements e.g. ²He went to ³schoo¹l.

   (b) Commands, e.g. ²Go to the ³doo¹r.

   (c) Requests, e.g. ²Please close the ³doo¹r.

   (d) Question-word question, e.g. ²Why did he ³lea¹ve?

   (e) Attached question, e.g. ²He didn't sleep, ³di¹d he?

2. *Pattern 233* (rising intonation) is used:

   (a) With yes–no questions: e.g. ²Do you ³like ³milk? ²Are ³you go³ing?

   (b) Questions with statement word order: e.g. ²It's ³time for ³class? ²You're ³not read³y?

As for Arab learners of English, intonation is, perhaps, the most difficult area to master, for various reasons. In the first place, because English language teachers are exclusively Arabs whose spoken English is sometimes weak, pupils are not exposed to genuine spoken English. An Arab learner transfers his old habit of Arabic intonation into English. In an Arabic utterance, there are more primary contours than in an English one, so an Arab learner tends to pronounce English with a staccato beat after the manner of Arabic stress and intonation.

The following two examples show the difference between English and Arabic intonation:

English: The ²boy went to the ³marke¹t.

Arabic: ða ha ba lw al a du 'ila ssuuqi: ذهب الولد إلى السوق
         3 2 2 3   2   2 3 1

This distributional feature of Arabic intonation makes Arab learners tend to over-use intonational contours in English. However, constant imitation and practice will improve the pupils' intonation.

---

[1] Pitch is the tone or the relative height of the voice. It has four degrees in English as follows:

(a) The lowest level, marked as ↘ e.g. She came yesterday. ↘

(b) The middle or normal level, marked as → or ↘ e.g. Good pupils → obey their teachers. ↘

(c) The high level, usually for the most important word in the unit of speech, or to mark the end of a yes–no question, marked as ↗, e.g. Can you answer it? ↗

(d) The very high level found in excited speech-anger, surprise, delight, etc.

4.9

Special Problems

Because English spelling is not regular, Arab learners encounter a problem in the phonological structure of some English words which results in poor pronunciation. The following are the most important problems that may face an Arab learner of English.

(a) *Orthography vs. Pronunciation:* Because Arabic is for the most part phonetically represented, an Arab pupil finds a problem in the phonological structure of sight words. Thus a pupil who has not heard or practised words like 'enough, though, through, cough and hiccough', is likely to make mistakes through false analogy because the visual configuration of such words is misleading.

The same problem is found with 'double o': words such as look, took, book, shook, good, wood, which are commonly pronounced with an /u/ sound; whereas other 'double o' words such as too, food, mood, shoot and moon are usually pronounced with an /uː/ sound.

A third type of these sight words are those which have an initial position /n/ sound with different spellings such as: knot, gnu, mnemonic and pneumonia. Under the influence of Arabic, an Arab learner of English often mispronounces such words.

(b) *Homophones:* as in 'sight words', an Arab pupil is likely to mispronounce brown/shown, now/mow, imply/simply, présent/presént, cónduct/condúct, etc.

(c) *Homographs:* the same problem is confronted with words which have similar spellings, but are pronounced differently. Examples: cow/slow, brown/shown, now/mow, imply/simply, présent/presént, cónduct/condúct, etc.

(d) *The Plural Form:* the plural morphs sometimes present a problem to an Arab learner of English as they confuse /s/ and /z/ or /ɪz/. These phonological patterns are conditioned by the sound that immediately precedes them. Thus, the ending is pronounced /s/ when the simple form ends in a voiceless consonant sound (other than a sibilant sound: /s/, /z/, /ʃ/, /ʒ/, /tʃ/, or /dʒ/.): /f/, /k/, /p/, /θ/, /h/, etc. Examples: books, maps, baths, etc.

The ending is pronounced /z/ when the simple form ends in a vowel or a voiced consonant sound (except the sibilants): /b/, /d/, /g/, /m/, etc. Examples: ribs, beds, lives, etc.

The ending is pronounced as a separate syllable (ɪz) when the final sound of the singular noun is a sibilant (i.e. hissing) sound. Examples: churches, glasses, bushes, fezes, etc.

(e) *Verbs: Present and Past forms.* The principles governing the pronunciation of third person present singular forms of verbs are the same as those for the pronunciation of regular plural nouns. Examples:

/s/	/z/	/ɪz/
looks	runs	passes
lets	robs	pushes
hopes	bathes	catches

The /t/ sound of the past tense form occurs after all unvoiced consonants except /t/; and /d/ allomorph occurs after all vowels and all voiced consonants except /d/; whereas the /ɪd/ sound occurs only after the sounds /t/ and /d/. Examples:

/t/	/d/	/ɪd/
kicked	showed	heated
laughed	leaned	wanted
stopped	killed	needed
wished	raised	decided

The English language teacher is expected to be aware of such problematic words so as to overcome the inconsistency of sound–symbol correspondence. And it is necessary for him to have contrastive knowledge of the Arabic and English sound systems in order to be able to predict problems before they occur.

4.10

Procedures and Techniques

The time available for pronunciation instruction in a typical English language lesson is often limited to the minimum. The teacher thus has to remedy his pupils' pronunciation through identifying their most common problems and giving them practice exercises and activities, rather than rules.

Furthermore, the teacher should design pronunciation drills and learning activities that will elicit pupil responses. For preliminary work the teacher may start with minimal-pair drills which are very useful for initial ear-training; but later, with advanced students, pronunciation work may be done within the context of communicative activites.

The best method of teaching the sound system (whether segmentals or supra-segmentals) is repetition and imitation. That is, the teacher says something and the pupils imitate him. However, after initial training, pronunciation drills can be contextualized so that repetition drills may become essential to real communication in the language. Situations and activities should be meaningfully related to pupils' interests or experience and the exercise materials are to be natural and realistic.

The following procedures are generally considered effective in teaching pronunciation to Arab learners of English.

Segmentals

1. The first step is to identify the pronunciation problem. The teacher introduces it to the class to focus the pupils' attention on the teaching point. In this respect, it is desirable to present one segmental phoneme each time so as not to confuse pupils.

2. The teacher writes on the blackboard a list of words that contain the target sound. Minimal pairs are one way of doing this. After that, he conducts an oral drill. He gives the model pronunciation, and pupils respond together and individually. The teacher says the words in pairs and the pupils repeat after him.

3. For pronunciation drills, the teacher may use props, explanatory diagrams, signals, tape-recorder or language laboratory, special charts or any other useful technique.

4. The teacher puts some of the given minimal pairs into phrases and sentences. He may give three short sentences for each minimal pair and ask pupils about the sounds they can hear. Once the pupils recognize and

identify the new sound, they must try to produce it, first in separate words and phrases, then in sentences, and finally in communicative utterances.

Let us assume, for example, that the teacher's assessment of pronunciation problems reveals that pupils need to work on the /ɪ/ and /e/ sounds in central position. To drill pupils in these phonemes, the teacher first offers the class some oral models containing the target segments in order to help pupils identify and discriminate between the two sounds. For this purpose he can conduct minimal pair drills, the commonest technique for aural identification. The teacher may model the pairs as follows:

/ɪ/	/e/
fill	fell
lit	let
sit	set
till	tell
will	well
bit	bet
wit	wet
pin	pen

The pupils mimic the teacher's (or the model's) pronunciation; and as soon as they can identify and discriminate the target sound, the teacher moves to the next step which is the use of such words in short utterances like:

to rest in bed
sit well
with help
felt ill
It fits well
Bring the dress
His friend is sick, etc.

Pupils repeat each pattern chorally and then individually after the model. During this activity, the teacher corrects bad utterances or unacceptable intonation immediately, or else pupils' pronunciation will become distorted.

To check pupils' perception of the target phoneme, the teacher may use the following techniques:

1. He gives a word from either list of the minimal pairs, and pupils (chorally or individually) say the contrasting word, e.g., Teacher: bit, Pupils: bet, etc.

2. Another technique of testing is to ask the class whether these sentences sound the same or different:
   1. He bit me.   He beat me.   (different)
   2. Ali beats me.   Ali beats me.   (same)
   3. Did he live?   Did he leave?   (different)

3. A short dialogue using the target sounds is to be memorized, e.g.
   A. Did she see it?
   B. No, she didn't see it.

Minimal pair drills are not sufficient in teaching pronunciation because pupils, especially in the early stages, have practised with words they don't know or are of little use to them since they are selected to remedy only problematic sounds. Even the phrases and sentences are not communicative.

Pupils, therefore, must learn to produce the target phoneme in meaningful contexts.

One of the easiest ways of having pupils practise sentences (containing the target sound) in a meaningful context is to ask them questions which stimulate responses containing the troublesome sound under study. For example to practise with the phonemes /s/ and /z/ the teacher may construct a drill like the following:

Teacher	:	Ask Salem if he reads a newspaper every day.
Pupil	:	Salem, do you read a newspaper every day?
Salem	:	No, I don't.
Pupil	:	No, Salem doesn't read a newspaper every day.
Teacher	:	Ask Ali what kind of fruit he likes.
Pupil	:	Ali what kind of fruit do you like?
Ali	:	Melons.
Pupil	:	He likes melons.

A variation of this drill is a contradiction drill in which pupils are required to correct a statement which contains an item of misinformation. Example: practising /s/ and /z/ phonemes.

Teacher	:	Saudi Arabia has one of the highest rainfalls in the world.
Pupil	:	No, it hasn't. It has one of the lowest rainfalls in the world.
Teacher	:	Syria doesn't have any mountains.
Pupil	:	Yes, it does. It has a lot of mountains.

Other types of pronunciation drills can be presented as classroom or group work activities. In such communicative activities, the pupils' attention is focused on conveying a message rather than on practising sounds in isolation. This feature is important because as soon as the pupils' attention is diverted to the content of the message when communicating in the language, native language influence reappears to produce a heavy speech accent. However, this type of learning activity requires careful design and preparation on the part of the teacher so that he can provide the pupils with experience in the pronunciation of English.

As a pedagogical strategy the English language teacher may follow these procedures:

1. First, he introduces the problematic pronunciation point, followed by representative examples for repetition.

2. After that, he gives the pupils clear instructions and demonstrations of how to practise the communication activity that incorporates the target phoneme(s).

3. When giving the necessary directions, the teacher pairs the class or organizes them into appropriate small groups to work on the activity. The teacher supervises the activities of the groups or offers help to whoever needs it.

4. The class reunites when the activity time is over. The pupils then present their decisions or reports on the activity so that the teacher can judge whether or not they have understood the pronunciation point.

These guidelines are illustrated by the following example:

Activity aim: To help pupils recognize those words which function as both nouns and verbs.

Method: The teacher explains that some English words function as both nouns and verbs although they have the same spelling. As a noun they are accented on the first syllable, but as a verb the stress is on the second syllable. After that he asks the pupils to listen to the pronunciation of some noun-verb pairs. The pupils listen and repeat after the teacher; conduct, export, conflict, contrast, convert. After this aural discrimination exercise, the teacher asks the class to work, in pairs or small groups, on the meaning of the nouns and verbs in given sentences. Timing is important in this regard so the teacher should give only the time required for practising the activity. Following this step, the teacher asks individual pairs or groups to explain the meaning of the given words to the class.

The activity may include sentences like the following:

1. The usher will conduct you to your seat in the cinema. However, if you display bad conduct the usher will show you the door.

2. A number of Arab countries export oil. Oil is a very important export of Arabia.

3. Ali has a conflict in his timetable. Thus his English lesson, given at 10 a.m. conflicts with history given at the same time.

4. Hana is a Muslim convert. Two years ago he decided to convert to the Islamic faith.

5. The Kuwaitis often contrast their present life with their previous one. Now they live in modern, well furnished houses, and have good education and medical treatment. The contrast between their former life and their present one is striking.

Other variations can be designed to teach different points of English pronunciation. However, the teacher is advised to consult specialized books of English pronunciation to choose exercises and activities that help pupils acquire the speech sounds of English.

Suprasegmentals

In teaching intonation and stress variation in speech, the teacher may use the following technique:

1. He writes on the chalkboard a simple sentence using vocabulary the students have already learned.

2. Then he draws attention to the teaching point and gives the necessary linguistic information for meaningful practice.

3. After that, he reads the sentence as it would normally be spoken.

4. It is desirable to indicate on the blackboard intonation lines, or numbers 1–4, or to indicate up or down arrows at the end of the sentence (↗ ↘).

5. Pupils repeat.

6. The teacher then gives aural exercises in discrimination. He may change

the place of stress or one of the function words within the sentence in order to produce phonemic difference. For example, a change in the intonation of a declarative sentence can transform it into a question:

Teacher	:	She's in hospital.
Pupil	:	Statement.
Teacher	:	She's in hospital?
Pupil	:	Question.

Placing stress (or emphasis) on different parts of a sentence results in phonemic difference, as in this example:

(a) Did
she go to school yesterday? (or her sister)

(b) Did she go to school
yesterday? (or last week)

(c) Did she go to
school yesterday? (or to the beach)

The teacher may conduct intonation or stress practice in the following way:
He writes a sentence on the blackboard e.g., 'We've won every volley-ball game in the last five weeks.' (The aim is practice on stress and on the phonemes /v/ and /w/) The teacher instructs a pupil to say the sentence with stress on *five*, and another pupil to say it with stress on *volleyball*, and a third one to say it with stress on *won*.

Once the pupils can distinguish the placement of stress on different parts of a sentence, they move on to practise intonation with short dialogues.

Dialogues offer excellent practice material in the rendering of stress, rhythm juncture and above all in practising oral fluency. If a sentence is uttered incorrectly, pupils are to repeat it two or three times until they master the required intonation before going on to the next sentence.

Chapter Five

Teaching Vocabulary

Introduction

Learning vocabulary is a lengthy and complex process which requires adequate mastery of form, meaning and usage. Through this process, the pupils should be able to: (i) spell and pronounce the words correctly when they use them either in writing or speaking, (ii) understand without difficulty the meaning of the words upon hearing or reading them, (iii) know the correct collocation of vocabulary as well as its connotations or associations, (iv) use vocabulary in appropriate grammatical sentences or utterances, knowing under what circumstances it occurs, the relationships between interlocutors, and the mode of the discourse – spoken or written, etc.

These requirements for knowing vocabulary are essential in foreign language learning because any ineffective vocabulary teaching and learning may lead to undesirable results such as:

(a) inability to retrieve learnt vocabulary while communicating in the language;

(b) inappropriate use of the vocabulary items in different situations as in the underlined words of the following sentences:
   – My car was badly <u>injured</u> in the accident. (damaged)
   – We shall <u>discuss</u> about the problem. (talk)
   The choice of words is as important as knowing their meanings, since what is correct in one situation may not be correct in another.

(c) ignorance of varieties of language. That is, using vocabulary at the wrong level of formality either of situation or the relationship between the speakers of the language.

(d) using bookish English (i.e. formal language found in textbooks) in normal conversational situations, e.g. the <u>hind</u> tyre of my car is worn out; so I must <u>purchase</u> a new one (hind/rear, purchase/buy or get).

(e) using vocabulary in a meaningless or in an unidiomatic way. For example: Her name is familiar <u>with</u> me (to).

(f) incorrect use of grammatical form, stress, pronunciation and spelling.

Examples: Words of different forms but of identical pronunciation such as genes/jeans, two/too, knight/night, in/inn, none/nun; or words of similar forms but pronounced differently, such as: wood/mood, book/food, bough/tough, through/hiccough, or words that function both as verb and noun such as 'record (noun)/re'cord (verb).

Thus the process of teaching/learning vocabulary requires good planning, effective presentation, demonstration and adequate practice.

5.1
Difficulties in Learning Vocabulary

The teaching of English vocabulary to monolingual Arab learners presents additional difficulty to the teacher because Arabic and English are not cognate languages. Both have different syntactic systems and word-formations; so the teacher will not have the advantage of cognates which might facilitate his task of teaching new lexical items. The teacher has to pay special attention to the form and sound of new items which are different from those of Arabic phonemes.

To overcome the problems associated with teaching English vocabulary to Arab pupils, a teacher's book is published to provide detailed guidelines of how to teach individual words. This book includes all the new items and structures.

There are, however, two major issues that influence the effectiveness of teaching English vocabulary to Arab pupils. One relates to the competence of the English language teacher, while the other is associated with the communication-oriented approach which is widely used in Arab countries.

The teacher is confronted with the problem of catering for the great number of vocabulary items included in the English syllabus. A competent teacher can provide a useful explanation followed by adequate practice. Unfortunately, this is not the case with many teachers. Empirical evidence indicates that teachers encounter difficulty in using the new vocabulary in appropriate contexts. This often happens when the teacher is new, inexperienced, inadequately trained or lacks fluency in spoken English. Apart from incorrect rhythm and intonation, mistakes can be observed with teachers using weak forms, idioms and structures. Pupils will not be able to communicate in English satisfactorily unless efforts are made to overcome these problems.

Communication-oriented teaching has also added a further load to the teacher's task. Thus, he is required to give his pupils, along with the language functions and notions, adequate English vocabulary to enable them to communicate effectively in the language. In addition, the teacher is required to contextualize all teaching points through the use of audio-visual aids, stories, etc.

The Teacher's Book used in Kuwaiti schools is inadequate in this respect as it does not give an appropriate meaning to each new vocabulary item. Instead, the meaning is left to the discretion of the teacher who usually resorts to translation. The result will be, of course, ineffective teaching and learning of the target language.

5.2

Types of vocabulary

In teaching English vocabulary, the FL teacher has to distinguish five types of vocabulary, namely: ESP (English for Special Purposes); active/productive; passive/receptive; function/structure; and content vocabulary. Although this classification is arbitrary, it is useful for pedagogical purposes. Some overlapping relationships exist between these types. ESP is related to special interests whether professional or technical. Its vocabulary helps the learners to enlarge their use of the content words. It is best learned in connection with the job or profession itself. However, in the classroom situation, pupils have to learn the forms and to understand the concepts behind words away from a real situation.

Productive (or active) vocabulary is utilized in everyday speech. It is learned for performance in any communication act. Hence, active words should be taught through focusing on the pronunciation, correct form, appropriate collocation and meaning so that pupils can easily remember them.

On the other hand, passive vocabulary is not essential for production in speaking or writing. It is meant for recognition and understanding. This vocabulary is needed for comprehension. The pupils are not asked to utilize it in everyday speech but recognize it when occurring in context. It may be added that words which are passive in a certain situation or level can be considered active in another context. This feature is not made clear in some English textbooks since all types of vocabulary are treated equally. To overcome this drawback, the teacher has to concentrate on the most useful items for the pupils. He should then handle the remaining items as receptive vocabulary to help improve pupils' recognition and comprehension.

Active and passive vocabulary are usually called content words because they carry lexical meaning in themselves.

Content words are closely related to one's experience. They are also open-ended in the sense that new nouns, verbs, adjectives and adverbs are often coined to name new things or processes.

Structure or function words are considered as part of the grammatical system of the language since their main functions are grammatical.

Unlike content words, structure words are limited in number. There are about two hundred of them in English. They belong to a closed class to which no new words can be added. Their meaning is mainly derived from the functions they serve. In other words, they are inseparable from content words in communication. For example, a string of content words like 'repairman find air conditioner broken' has no grammatical relationship between its elements; but with some structure words we can bring it to grammaticality in this form: 'The repairman found the air conditioner broken', and thus the whole message is conveyed. If we examine the structure word 'do' in the sentence 'Do you always walk on the beach at sunset?' We find that its main function is grammatical because it serves as a marker of the question form and as a marker of tense.

Function words are also used:

(a) to join fragments of structures together into larger units as with prepositions.

(b) to join pairs of sentences or phrases as in co-ordinating conjunctions: but, yet, and, or, nor, and for.

(c) to connect a subordinate idea to the main sentence as with subordinating conjunctions: if, although, because, whenever, since, until, etc.

(d) as a sequence signal as with the article 'the' which can be used as an anaphoric reference, i.e. a reference to something which has been previously mentioned. For example: An old man was standing at the door. The old man left before one.

Function words have high frequency in the language. That is, words like 'the', 'a', 'in', 'that' or the auxiliaries and conjunctions occur very frequently in any piece of writing in order to establish the grammatical structure of sentences. However, they are unstressed in spoken language which makes them difficult for a foreign language learner to identify.

5.3
Word Form

English and Arabic are not cognate languages and each has a different syntactic system and word-formation. There are certain English borrowings in colloquial Arabic (e.g. radio, cinema, computer, telephone, etc.) But these are exceptions. Arab learners of English do not have the advantage of cognate features or similarities in the alphabet, spelling, pronunciation, derivation, affixes, and the like. This has to be taken into consideration when teaching English vocabulary to Arab pupils. This is not an easy task for the teacher. He has to describe the lexical items that manifest:

(a) internal change in form, e.g., man-men, foot-feet, sing-sung, ride-rode, etc.

(b) external change in form, e.g., happy, happiness, happily, or kind, kindness, kindly, etc.

(c) both internal and external changes in form, e.g. maintain, maintenance, explain, explanation, explanatory, etc.

(d) no change in form but a difference in function, e.g. sheep as singular or plural, record as noun or verb.

The process of word formation is an effective aid to vocabulary building. Teaching experience indicates that systematic presentation and practice of selected affixes enable pupils to learn an entire system of vocabulary rather than individual words.[1] The teacher should exploit the lexical characteristics of English to help his pupils make greater use of varied vocabulary. He should make every effort to teach derivational forms or affixes that may be attached to a word.

Knowledge of affixes will help pupils (a) derive new words from already known ones, (b) increase their ability to utilize the vocabulary system, (c) grapple with derived words when they are presented for the first time, (d) understand the basic meaning of other related words if their root is familiar to them, e.g. define (root word), definition, definable and redefine, (e) be aware of the correlation between various affixes and their functions and meanings; e.g., -tion signalling a noun, -able an adjective, -ly an adverb of manner, un- signalling not, re- signalling again, etc. and (f) improve their spelling skill especially in affixes.

[1] Affixes is a general term that denotes:
(a) prefix, an affix added to the beginning of a word, e.g. *un*able, *re*place, *super*market, etc.
(b) infix, an affix added inside the root, e.g. ride-r*o*de, goose-g*ee*se, etc.
(c) suffix, an affix added to the end of a word, e.g. discover*y*, act*or*, etc.

However, it is not enough to know the affixes to predict the function or the meanings of the words they are added to. For example, not all words ending in -al are adjectives as there are other words like revival or denial which function as nouns. Also, the prefix dis-, meaning negation or reversal, does not help in understanding the relationship between appoint and disappoint as the latter does not mean 'to remove from an appointed position'. Consequently, the teacher must teach derived words in appropriate contexts so that their meanings become clear to the pupils. However, the teacher is not encouraged to teach many derivatives of a single word stem if this leads to confusion.

Related to derivatives is word association. In introducing new items of vocabulary, the teacher must draw the pupils' attention to the verbs or nouns that are usually accompanied by certain prepositions. This combination changes the basic meaning of the word as in 'look for', 'look out', 'look up', 'look after', etc. These prepositions should be memorized along with the verb or noun they are associated with.

Furthermore, care should be taken when dealing with those forms that exhibit changes both in spelling and pronunciation like 'explain – explanatory', 'inflame – inflammatory', 'severe – severity', etc. The same care is to be given to those forms that have phonological differences when pronounced.

In addition, there are other word formation processes that produce new forms such as compounds, blends, clipped forms and acronyms. Compounds are formed by two or more individual words, and they can be written as one unit. That is, one word such as football and blackboard, or hyphenated such as finger-print, night-dress and brother-in-law, or as separate words like day nursery, day labourer and prime minister.

5.4

Word Frequency Lists

To facilitate learning English as a foreign language, linguists as well as educators have compiled lists of vocabulary items on a frequency basis, believing that such word counts would be:

(a) useful in selecting and controlling active vocabulary;

(b) useful in preparing instructional material in order to teach more common words before unusual or rare ones;

(c) adequate for oral or written communication;

(d) and above all, effective in simplifying the learning of the language.

One of the well known lists is the General Service List designed by Michael West in 1953. It consists of 2000 common words extracted from some five million words. It takes into account not only forms but also lexical items. That is, the different meanings of the same word and the idiomatic usage related to it are also listed. This word count has appended to it a specialized word list of 425 technical and scientific words.

A more recent word list was compiled in 1964 by Brown University in the United States. It consists of over 50,000 words belonging to fifteen fields of study such as mathematics, philosophy, literature, history, etc.

Other important frequency counts are:

(a) The Teacher's Word Book of 30,000 words, produced by Edward L. Thorndike and Irving Lorge in 1944. The list is considered now a generation out of date as it does not include modern words of high frequency.

(b) The American Heritage Word Frequency Book assembled by John B. Caroll, Peter Davis and Barry Richman, in 1971.

(c) Pranisskas' specialized lists (1972) drawn up from ten textbooks used by first-year university students.

(d) A Spoken Word Count compiled by Joseph M. Wepman and Wilbur Hass, in 1966 for adults, and in 1969 for children aged 5 to 7. (See Robinett, 1978.)

These lists have a common core of about 1,500 items along with the structural words which are extremely important for written or spoken communication irrespective of subject. They also reveal whether or not words that occur frequently have been included in teaching materials. The differences among them, however, are due to the nature of the counted materials or to the goals of teaching. Thus if the specific purpose is to teach scientific English, then the list will have an obvious bias towards technical vocabulary, and if the objective is to develop speaking or writing skills, the list will involve the words that serve either purpose.

Despite their merits, word counts can be misleading because they do not specify the different meanings of the words of the same form. That is, any words spelled the same way are often counted as the same word regardless of their different meanings.

For example, a word like ruler is described in the vocabulary counts (except the General Service List) as one form though it can refer to a measuring stick or to a person who governs. Moreover, the meaning of ruler remains ambiguous unless the context and situation is made clear.

It happens also that some words are of great usefulness in particular situations but have a very low frequency and are not even included in the word lists. For example, the words chalk and blackboard are very useful in classroom situations. However, the former i.e. chalk does not appear frequently in the General Service List while the latter is not mentioned at all. As a result, frequency need not be the only criterion for vocabulary selection or teaching as there are other criteria for word priority such as:

(a) Appropriateness. Some words may be taught or learned first because they are seen as functional in some situations or specific settings as in English for special purposes – ESP.

(b) Utility. Useful words have priority in teaching or learning vocabulary regardless of their nature or level of difficulty.

(c) Immediacy. Words that are related to pupils' immediate needs or environment have priority in teaching whether they are concrete or abstract, regular or irregular, in or outside school.

(d) Frequency. Common (or cognate) words like man, boy, girl, big, small, bus, cycle, microbe, etc., are usually taught before unusual ones like polymorphic, gigantic, sociopolitical, etc.

(e) Simplicity. This criterion is relative, because it happens that a lexical item like submarine is easier to teach than a familiar form like head. The former has only one meaning whereas the latter has several.

However, simplicity depends on several variables most important of which are the following:

(a) Word structure. A monosyllabic word is usually easier to learn than a multi-syllabic form.

(b) Phonological structure. Words that are phonetically represented like sit, door, swim, car are easier to spell and pronounce than words that do not show correspondence between their graphemes and phonemes like through, enough, knowledge, yacht, restaurant, etc.

(c) Nature of the word. Concrete words are more easily taught than abstract forms or concepts.

(d) Similarity. Cognate or borrowed forms can be easily grasped since they have similarities in pronunciation and meaning. Also, words that contain phonemes similar to those in Arabic are easier to learn than words that have different phonemes.

5.5

Word Meaning

A meaning of a word is difficult to grasp because it may change from one situation or context to another. This can be illustrated with the word 'table', which has different meanings according to the context and to its position in the sentence.

Table:

- There is usually a table and a chair for the teacher in each classroom (a piece of furniture).
- There is often a timetable in each classroom (times of classes/subjects and their times).
- He amused the whole table by his funny jokes (people sitting at a table).
- The table does not include codes or symbols (information arranged in the form of a list).
- Where is the boss? He is at table (having a meal).
- Some candidates pay voters under the table (money given in order to influence people dishonestly).
- During cross-examination, the defendant turned the tables on the accuser (seized a position of strength).

It is clear from the above examples that the particular meaning of the lexical form depends upon which situation it is being associated with. The English language teacher should take this into consideration when teaching new vocabulary. This is especially the case with common words, as most of them have a wide denotative range, contrary to technical forms which usually have a specific meaning. The teacher, therefore, must avoid teaching the meaning from lists of unrelated words. Instead he should concentrate on appropriate contexts so as to make the connotational meaning of a word clear and easier to learn. Moreover, all different uses of each structure word should be taught.

Cultural information is closely associated with meaning. The customs, beliefs, and all the other products of the people of the target language constitute an essential part of the lexical system reflected in the collocations of words. When introducing or explaining new vocabulary, the teacher should not neglect such cultural insights; otherwise an important aspect of the lexical meaning will be lost to the detriment of foreign language learning.

5.6

Types of Meaning

There are at least four kinds of meaning which can be differentiated when discussing the semantic content of word forms. They are: lexical, grammatical, connotational and idiomatic meaning.

1. Lexical Meaning

This type is often called the dictionary or denotational meaning which is common to all speakers of the same language. It does not change from one situation to another. Nor is it affected by personal experience. Pupils can learn it by connecting the form with the category of things that often accompany it. For example, the meaning of the abstract word 'devoted' can be specified by a list of associated words and ideas as follows:

> He is a devoted father
> She is a devoted wife
> He is devoted to his work
> She is devoted to her boss/company, children, etc.

When teaching such vocabulary, the teacher must cultivate the pupils' awareness of any specific lexical items that are associated with it.

2. Grammatical Meaning

Grammatical meaning is essential for understanding the language. It is determined by the syntactic relationships within the language or by grammatical signals. The following are two examples:

(1) The girl hit the cat yesterday.
(2) The cat hit the girl yesterday.

The lexical meaning of the items girl, hit and cat is the same in both sentences; yet the grammatical meaning of girl and cat is different because of their relationship with the verb 'hit'. In the first sentence 'girl' is the doer of the action and the subject of the sentence. In contrast it is the receiver of the action in the second, because it bears a different relationship to the verb 'hit'. But if the main verb is 'saw', and not 'hit' in the first utterance, the item 'girl' will have the grammatical meaning of experiencer rather than the performer due to the peculiar properties of the verb 'saw' which are different from those of the verb 'hit'.

It is clear that grammatical signals such as: the, his, a/an, many, several, etc. control meaning and help in discovering the exact meaning of the word. Pupils, therefore, should be taught the skill of recognizing these signals by giving them useful exercises and drills practising awareness of the grammatical environment of the word like the following:

> There _____ twenty-eight pupils in my class.
> The defendant was _____ ed several questions.
> The _____ was responsive to the teacher's _____.
> Success requires some _____, etc.

Intonation and inflections are also determinants of grammatical meaning. They will be discussed in some detail in the following chapter which deals with grammar teaching.

3. Connotational Meaning

Knowing the lexical and grammatical meaning is not always enough to communicate accurately and appropriately in the target language. There is also the meaning which is related to the culture of the target language. This meaning is an essential part of the total semantic system. Some words or phrases are associated with special connotations or interpretations which have evolved from personal experiences. Hence, connotational meaning is subjective, unlike the objective denotational (i.e. lexical) meaning, because it carries with it personal feelings, judgement or experiences. For example, the behaviour of a person may seem to some people 'sociable, polite or good'. Yet the same behaviour can be judged by other people as 'awkward, ruthless or bad' according to their personal interpretations or experience.

Word association is another aspect of connotation although it is related more to the individual or to culture. For example, the connotation of the word dog may differ from one person or community to another. These different interpretations result from personal experiences or social attitudes, and they must be taken into account if accurate communication is sought.

However, such cultural insights create a problem to Arab learners of English. English language teachers rarely explain the cultural content or connotational meaning when introducing new vocabulary. In other words, teachers tend to focus on the denotational or lexical meaning at the expense of cultural understanding.

4. Idiomatic Meaning

Idioms, proverbs and clichés constitute an integral part of language and are extensively used. Pupils must therefore learn them as part of the vocabulary system.

First of all, idioms and their variations, phrasal and prepositional verbs are frequently encountered by pupils, so they must be taught as individual lexical items. However, idioms, a special form of collocation, give rise to a problem in learning because they often carry cultural content with them. Their meaning is also vague and cannot be understood from the individual words. That is, the literal meaning of the words does not contribute much to comprehension of the expression. For example, the phrase 'It was raining cats and dogs' means that it rained heavily, not cats and dogs which have no connection with raining (Collins 1961, p. 14).

Nevertheless, some idioms are less difficult than others because their meanings are more transparent. Examples include: look for (try to find), have the upper hand (be in control), keep someone in the dark (not tell someone anything), put forward (suggest) and give up (stop doing something).

Other problems confronting the teaching of idioms are: (a) the difficulty of grouping them in specific categories, and (b) the difficulty of recognizing what idioms can undergo changes, as some of them do not alter their structure. For example, the expression 'turn a deaf ear' cannot be made passive. It would be ridiculous to say 'a deaf ear has been turned or will be turned, etc.' But some changes are possible. For example, we could say 'keep in touch, he has been in touch, he will be in touch, etc.'.

In teaching such expressions it is more effective to indicate what changes the idiom can undergo. In addition, the teacher has to present them as individual lexical items and to teach them in appropriate relevant contexts.

Like idioms, *multi-word verbs* have a special meaning that is different from the meanings of the individual words they contain.[1] They are also used frequently. However, they pose some problems for the pupils, such as choosing the right particle (i.e. preposition or adverb) for the verb, and how to stress the new pattern. In addition some of these structural units or collocations cannot be made passive. It would be odd, for instance, to say 'He was arrived in London'. But it is possible to say 'The baby was looked after' and so on.

Multi-word verbs should be taught in the same way as other idioms, that is as individual lexical items, and in realistic contexts in order to illustrate other meanings. However, it is helpful to group them in categories such as break away, break into, break off, break out, break up, break down, etc.

Clichés are a special form of expression. Their meanings however, are often more transparent than those of idioms or proverbs. For example, an Arab learner can recognize without much difficulty what is meant by: so far so good, first and foremost, as strong as an ox, as white as snow, etc. Such expressions form a part of the vocabulary system and are frequently used in conversation, and, as in other areas of vocabulary, the teaching of clichés should be done in appropriate situations. It may be noted that they are often taught for recognition and not necessarily for production.

Proverbs are also an important part of the language and culture that pupils should learn. There is, however, no specific strategy for teaching proverbs; but whenever pupils come across a proverb, the teacher is required to explain its general meaning, the moral statements it involves, and the context it is usually used in.

5.7

Presentation of Meaning

There are various ways of explaining the meaning of a word, most important of which are the following:

1. Demonstration
This technique involves:

(a) Direct association. In this procedure, a new word is taught by the direct association of its reference whether a real object or a picture of that object. This technique is preferable for young learners or for words referring to concrete objects available in the classroom or school environment.

(b) Acting. The teacher may dramatize or mime the situation by means of gestures, dialogues or role-playing to help the pupils understand the meaning of a word. This technique is more applicable in items involving action or movement such as walking, writing, speaking, eating and the like.

(c) Word games. These are useful instruments for explaining and practising vocabulary. Among these games are crossword puzzles, word chains, category words and word-wheel puzzles. Word games can be used at all stages of learning.

---

[1] Multi-word verbs or structural units are of two kinds: phrasal verbs and prepositional verbs. Both are structured from a verb plus a particle (i.e. preposition or adverb like up, out, down, off, away, in, on, over, etc.) The main difference between them is that with phrasal verbs the particle is often separated from its associated verb. Examples: Call him up, put your hand down, look this word up, make it up, etc. Prepositional verbs, on the other hand are fused verbs, e.g.: bring about (= cause), bring up (= rear (children) or mention (a topic)), find out (= discover), etc.

2. Explanation

This technique consists of

(a) Description. The meaning of a new word is taught by describing and defining objects or referents. This can be done by limiting their class function, location, or qualities. The teacher may explain the words beforehand or as they arise. However, he must be careful not to overemphasize word explanations at the expense of other language activities or class time, as this approach will undermine the teaching strategy. He may leave some words for pupils to guess or infer their meanings from context. He should choose such words carefully, otherwise the process will be time-consuming. It is useful in this respect to explain to pupils how meaning can be deduced from context. The teacher may also encourage pupils to work out meaning for themselves by asking them to look up words in their dictionaries provided it does not take up too much of the class time.

(b) Synonyms and antonyms. The meaning of a word may be explained either by giving the semantic equivalent or opposite of the word. Examples: lorry and truck, stop and go, stand up and sit down, etc. However, the teacher should be very careful when employing this technique because:

    (i) the given meaning might be more difficult than the target word itself;

    (ii) not all synonyms or antonyms occur in the same situations or can be used in exactly the same way. Examples include: interchangeable words like lift and raise, bright and sharp, etc. Each of these forms has its own connotations or usage.

    (iii) some words have two different meanings, like old, young or new, light, dark or heavy; in these situations the teacher should explain to pupils which meaning of the word is intended.

(c) Translation. A new item can often be explained in simple words in the target language. This may not be true in some cases. The word cannot be elicited or its meaning is too difficult for students to understand. In these circumstances the teacher may resort to the mother tongue. This strategy of translation can save time especially at the early stages of learning the foreign language. However translation should not be used too often.

(d) Context. The presentation of vocabulary items around a topic or a centre of interest enhances the process of learning. This is especially the case if the teacher is following a communicative approach. However, the teacher should be careful in the choice of words or phrases to be explained and of the texts he utilizes for this purpose. Thus he should provide the students with short authentic texts, and ensure that they have understood the main points of the passage before discussing words and phrases which are supported by the context to see how they can be related to one another.

    There are several techniques that the teacher can employ in the teaching of vocabulary in context. Thus he may:

    (i) ask vocabulary questions about the target word so that students can elicit or guess its meaning. He may also ask the class questions such as: 'Does anyone know/understand the meaning of this word? Who knows the opposite of this word? Can you find another word in the passage which means ...?', or he may provide the class with the meaning of the word or phrase, then ask them to find the target word. In this respect he may help them find the required item by telling them in which paragraph or sentence it is, etc.

(ii) List words which are semantically related and discuss them together.

(iii) Analyse the internal structure of a word or a collocation and ask pupils to interpret its meaning, e.g.: breath-taking, dishonest;

(iv) Give related forms to the unknown item e.g.: act, actor, actress, acting;

(v) Ask pupils to find out words or phrases that show cause and effect, bad habits, etc.

Teaching such exercises requires a flexible, oral approach to make the lesson lively and interesting and to lead the students to a reasonable guess.

(e) Collocation. The teacher can discuss the meaning of new vocabulary by means of collocations. This technique is useful in teaching vocabulary because it arranges words that normally occur together. For example, the word car may involve some words that associate with it such as: driver, car accident, collide, traffic lights, garage, windscreen, headlight, steering wheel, brakes, etc. Other types of collocations are multi-word verbs i.e. phrasal verbs, some idioms, compound words (noun + noun, adjective + noun, verb + adverb, etc.), clichés and other expressions. Students should be encouraged to record or note down normal collocations they come across for memorization and retrieval.

3. Visual Aids

This method involves the use of photographs, drawings, maps, wall-pictures, flash cards, figures, slides, transparencies, video films, and other illustrations. The significance of these aids is that they present vocabulary in a visual context. One way of presenting new items through them is as follows:

1. Show some objects on a poster, or on a wall-picture, without any writing.
2. Say the words for each object aloud.
3. Show the mouth movements involved in saying the word.
4. Get students to familiarize themselves with the pronunciation.
5. Once the students are familiar with the vocabulary, point at the objects and ask the students to tell you what they are.
6. Show the written forms on the board.
7. Point at the objects again and get the students to read the corresponding word from the board.

5.8

Teaching Procedures

Teaching vocabulary does not stop with learning the meaning of a word. It continues until students learn how to use the word correctly in appropriate communicative acts or situations. However, there are some procedures the teacher should take into consideration when presenting the new lexical items. Here are some of the principles that are to be borne in mind:

(a) The teacher must identify the amount of vocabulary – active or passive – the students can learn. This is important because many new words might confuse students. However, the quantity of vocabulary or its type is usually decided for the teacher by the textbook he is using.

(b) Words should be presented in such a way that they make an impression on the students' minds. That is presentation should be vivid and motivating so as to make students feel that they need the new words.

(c) New vocabulary should be presented in appropriate situations or with the words they normally collocate with as well as with structural environmental signals, i.e. noun and verb signals or with associated prepositions or markers.

(d) Students should have a specific understanding of what the new word refers to. That is its denotation and connotation meanings have to be clear.

(e) There must be enough practice in the receptive use of the target words for the students to learn them. Repetition is also an effective technique especially for young learners. The teacher should check whether the pupils can recognize the new forms and identify their meanings.

(f) Students must practise the use of the new words, especially productive vocabulary, with the correct use of stress, pronunciation and meaning.

(g) The teacher should encourage students to record new vocabulary in their note-books for future use. The teacher may provide the class with the equivalent meaning in the mother tongue for each foreign word.

In addition, there are several ways to introduce new vocabulary items. The following are the most appropriate techniques applicable to any vocabulary in a reading lesson:

1. Recognition Stage

At this stage the teacher presents the phonic form, the graphic form, the lexical meaning and the grammatical position of each new word. He also demonstrates how to associate each new item with certain other words, ideas, functions and subject areas. In these situations the teacher:

1. First pronounces the word two or three times with the students listening. They may repeat the word after him if the need arises. A difficult word, however, should constantly be repeated.

2. Creates a situation, or uses an appropriate context or communicative language function to show how the new word is normally used. He may also ask questions related to the function of the target word or simply make a statement including the item under study.

3. Clarifies the meaning of the unknown item through definition, demonstration, visual aids, synonyms and antonyms, or even translation, or dictionary work.

4. Shows the visual form of the new word and its collocation. This can be done on the chalkboard or on flash cards so that students can recognize its spelling and visual configuration. If there is any spelling problem related to the target word, the teacher will draw the pupils' attention to it. The pupils may then write it down in their vocabulary books.

2. Receptive Stage

During this stage, the teacher provides the learners with exercises that stress reception rather than production which may further illustrate the meaning. Furthermore he presents language functions or exercises of different kinds of contexts in which the new item can be used so as to show the class its connotative meanings. Students should be aware of other meanings of the word they are trying to master especially if it is an active vocabulary item. At this stage, it is also necessary to check their understanding of the meaning. To do this the teacher may ask the students questions and their answers will determine whether or not they have understood the meaning of the relevant word.

3. Productive Stage

At this stage, the teacher will concentrate on how to use the newly learned word productively. For this purpose he has to provide the class with exercises that help students develop the ability to use the target word correctly in sentences. Students are requested to use it in situations or contexts. As an alternative technique the teacher may ask them questions, the answers to which require the use of the target word.

If inexperienced teachers have some difficulty in dealing with such exercises they should consult the Teacher's Book for the course they are using or else a general guide to teaching techniques.

5.9

Techniques for Creating Interest

In teaching new vocabulary the teacher needs to create interest so that the pupils can follow the presentation attentively and enthusiastically. External motivation is very important. Here are some suggestions for making the teaching interesting:

1. With regard to the form of words the teacher may use prefixes and suffixes to form as many words as possible with root words.
   Examples:

Product	:	products, production, productive, productivity, un-productive, producer, etc.
Direct	:	indirect, direction, directional, directions, directive, director, directorate, directory, etc.

2. He may scramble the letters of the new word. Thus the teacher first pronounces the word, then he writes the letters (out of order) on the chalkboard. Students are asked to rearrange the letters of the word in the right order.

3. The teacher may draw a picture on the blackboard, or show a figure of the referent. Students try to guess the relevant word and write it on the board. The teacher can make this exercise easier by giving the first or the last letter of the word for the pupils to complete it.

4. The teacher writes a lot of words on the chalkboard. Then as he quickly says one of the words on the board, a student must point to it.

5. The teacher may use the target word in an appropriate sentence. He writes the sentence on the blackboard and gives the class a number of simple cue-words which are normally associated with the target word. Then pupils try to guess the word by means of the cue-words, and underline it.

The Meaning of Words

The teacher can make his teaching of the meanings of words interesting in various ways:

1. He may ask students to give a single word for a specified meaning or phrase. *Examples:* – An electronic calculating machine that processes data and recalls information at very high speeds (computer). – A book or list of names, facts, or telephone numbers (directory).

2. If the teacher uses real objects, he can wrap them in a piece of cloth and let the pupils guess what the object is by feeling it.

3. The teacher can perform an action in such a way as to be slightly ambiguous, and the pupils guess what the meaning is.

4. The teacher gives the class a list of words and a list of meanings. Pupils connect each word on the list to its meaning with a line.

5. Another type of exercise is the use of memory. This activity is used for practising words that have already been introduced. The game goes like this: the teacher shows the students some objects or pictures for one minute, then he puts them away. The pupils write or say the names of as many of the objects as they can remember.

6. The teacher may use multiple-choice techniques. Example:
   Please _____ me a telegram.
   (a) receive   (b) buy   (c) send   (d) discuss

7. By using games or riddles such as those suggested below:
   (a) What do you do: to bread if you want to make sandwiches? – to a present if you don't want people to know what it is?
   (b) How is: a road when it has ice on it? a shoe if you wear it for too long? milk when you leave it for a long time?
   (c) What is it?
   You wear them to cover your legs.
   You read it in the newspaper when you want to buy something.
   You spin it to make a sweater.

8. Rearrangement of words into sentences is another technique to facilitate learning the specific items and their associates. Example: lesson, comprised, this, parts, of, is, five (This lesson is comprised of five parts).

9. As a variation of this exercise pupils are asked to match words in column *A* with words in columns *B* and *C* which are related in meaning. Example:

A	*B*	*C*
ice	blurred	flu
sneezing	melt	unfocused
photographs	symptoms	water etc.

The foregoing exercises give a good idea of just what has to be done to ensure learning on the part of the pupils. They are just a sample. The resourceful teacher can think of many more useful and practical exercises.

5.10

Exercises for Vocabulary Development

The best way of developing students' vocabulary is to give them a chance to encounter the language in authentic contexts, situations or exercises. The following examples are specimens of vocabulary exercises that are useful for vocabulary building. However, the English language teacher is requested to design his own exercises to help pupils increase and develop their vocabulary.

1. *Inference Exercises:* Here the teacher may present to his students short appropriate contexts containing the target words. Then he asks them to infer the meaning of these unknown words from the given contexts. Examples:

   (a) All the _____ has been completely spent and not a single penny is left for buying a sandwich (money).

   (b) The exhibition contains different types of _____: buses, cars, lorries, coaches, trams, bulldozers and cranes (vehicles).

   (c) The _____ you showed me yesterday is too large for my small family (villa or house).

2. *Synonym and Antonym Exercises:* This type of exercise can be misleading because not all synonyms or antonyms are interchangeable. For example border and frontier are not true synonyms since each has its own connotations. The teacher, therefore, should be careful not to give students confusing items when dealing with such exercises. Examples:

   (a) Synonyms:
       (i) I have never seen such a big elephant.
           It is really _____ (very large, huge).
       (ii) Indicate the synonyms of the underlined words:
           Familiar: close, intimate, fraternal, confidential, chummy.
           Annoy: irritate, bother, irk, vex, provoke, aggravate, peeve, rile.

   (b) Antonyms in brief contexts:
       (i) The two boys *resemble* each other in appearance, but they _____ in behaviour (differ).
       (ii) Our last boss was *mean*, but the newly appointed boss seems very _____. It is a pleasure to work with him (generous).
       (iii) I have *lent* Yousif another five dinars; that is the fourth time he has _____ money from me this month (borrowed).

   (c) Antonyms formed by using prefixes:
       Fill in the blanks with a word beginning with il-, im-, in-, ir-, un-, dis-, which is opposite in meaning:

A	B	
direct	_____	(in-)
logical	_____	(il-)
potent	_____	(im-)
regular	_____	(ir-)
honest	_____	(dis-)
happy	_____	(un-)

3. *Area of reference exercises:* These are useful for practising, revising and developing vocabulary. In such exercises students are asked to make word clusters (or groups or sets) or to match words with others with which they are most commonly used. Examples:

(a) *Word-sets:*

Politics	:	cabinet, parliament, minister, diplomacy, non-aligned, conference, etc.
Business	:	import/export, shareholders, stock market, capital, account, retail, etc.
Hospital	:	doctor, nurse, patient, operation, intensive care, surgery, etc.
Media	:	newspapers, television, radio, journals, periodicals, circulars, etc.

(b) Other useful exercises of area of reference are matching exercises. For example, students may be asked to match words, say, in column 'A' with others in column 'B':

A	B
ice	stop
police	cream
post	bag
exercise	station
bus	office
shopping	book

4. *Collocation Exercises:* Collocation is useful for learning vocabulary since it deals with words that normally occur together. Collocation exercises need not necessarily use difficult or passive vocabulary. One variation of collocation is a completion exercise. Examples:

a _____ of cigarettes
a _____ of tea
a _____ of beans
a _____ of wine
a _____ of matches, etc.

Another type of collocation exercise is the completion of expressions such as:

Swim like _____
Sharp as _____
Strong as _____
Weak as _____ etc.

5. *Scale Exercises:* In such exercises, students arrange given words either in ascending or descending order starting with the largest or smallest item. Examples:

(a) grape, lemon, orange, grapefruit.
(b) 5, 1, 3, 9, 6, 4, 7, 2, 8
(c) room, flat, house, factory.
(d) gale, wind, breeze, storm, hurricane, etc.

6. *Semantic Field Exercises:* These aim at establishing relationships between words in the general area of meaning. One type of such drills is to ask

students to give as many terms as they can, belonging to a certain category or area of meaning. For example, the teacher may ask the class to write down all the terms they know related to family relationships, mass media, sports, etc. As an example of family relationships, students may give words like: mother, father, son, daughter, brother, sister, parents, cousin, nephew, step-father, grandfather.

As a variation of this type of exercise, the teacher may provide the class with a picture or drawing of an object with numbers on specific parts. Then he asks students to list the target word for each number in the drawing. Suppose the teacher gives the students a drawing of the human body with certain numbers on it, the exercise then goes as follows:

Number in drawing	Term required
1	head
5	foot
10	eyes
3	nose
12	teeth
7	forehead
2	mouth
6	arm

7. *Compound Exercises:* Here the aim is to produce one form for compound phrases. For example, the form for the person who goes to a theatre is theatre-goer. What is the form for the person who

plays football	(football player)
teaches French	(French teacher)
pays taxes	(taxpayer)
drives a bulldozer	(bulldozer driver)
draws maps	(map drawer).

8. *Word-structure Exercises:* these exercises constitute an effective way of expanding vocabulary and a useful means of inferring word meaning. They involve the use of prefixes and suffixes attached to the root word. The teacher can employ such words in various ways. Thus he may ask students to work out the meaning of affixed forms either in context or by definition. Examples:

(a) Give the meaning of the underlined words:
   - He found a lot of misprints in the book
   - People usually dislike humid weather
   - She tried to pass the driving test, but she was unsuccessful.
   - One can buy almost anything one needs at a *supermarket*.

(b) Find the definition in column 'B' which matches the word in column 'A'.

A	B
trilogy	of, on, with two sides
polymath	able to speak many different languages
bilateral	series of three related books, plays, etc.
multilingual	a person with great skill in many branches of knowledge.

5.11

Vocabulary Games and Activities

Vocabulary games are essential to the learning process because they:
(a) give students a chance to revise the words they have already learned;
(b) vitalize learning;
(c) create a relaxed atmosphere in the classroom;
(d) motivate students to communicate in English;
(e) activate reluctant or unwilling students.

However, vocabulary games require, among other things, careful preparation and organization on the part of the teacher before presenting them to the class. In addition, the students should be aware of the aim of the activity and of the manner in which it is going to be conducted.

There are hundreds of vocabulary games of various levels, objectives and types. The teacher is advised to consult books dealing with such games to choose from them what best serves his teaching purpose. We list here some popular games for general consideration or orientation.

1. The teacher chooses a five-letter word such as, for example, *table*, and asks students to write it across the top, putting one letter above each of the five squares as shown in the diagram; then he asks them to write the words nouns, verbs, adjectives, adverbs down the lefthand side.[1]

	T	A	B	L	E
Nouns	teacher	answer	business	limit	event
Verbs	think	arrive	begin	leave	erase
Adjectives	tender	angry	busy	lazy	equal
Adverbs	thoroughly	anxiously	beautifully	luckily	evenly

2. One student thinks of an object available in the classroom. Then he asks the class what it is. He could say, for example, I can see (or think of) something beginning with 'M', What is it? (map).

3. A variation of this guessing game is 'Twenty Questions' which is well-known by language teachers. A student thinks of a person, object or event which the other students of the class have to guess within a limit of twenty questions.

4. Students are given a jumble of letter cards, on each card there is a letter of the target word. The task for students is to rearrange the letter-cards in the correct order. This activity is very useful for spelling.

5. This game is often called 'odd man out' or 'intruder'. The teacher provides the class with groups of words in the same semantic field but in each group there is one word which does not belong to the others. For example:

> silver, copper, wood, gold   (wood)
> traditional, old, modern, ancient   (modern)

The students must spot the intruders and explain why they do not belong.

6. This game is a useful activity. The students try to find as many words as they can, beginning at the top of the wheel and moving in a clockwise

[1] This game is quoted from *English Teaching Forum*, Vol. 7/6, 1969.

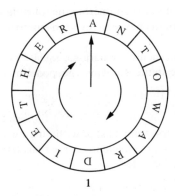 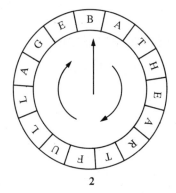

1 2

Possible yielded words are: (1) a, an, ant, to, tow, toward, war, ward, die, diet, ether, the, he, her, era, ran, rant: (2) bat, bath, bathe, a, at, the, he, hear, heart, ear, art, artful, full, age.

direction, as shown in the diagrams[1]

Other useful vocabulary activities are the following:

1. Finding antonyms or synonyms of known words.
2. Classifying words under appropriate categories, e.g. food, fruit, vegetables, animals, furniture, sports, relatives, flowers, etc.
3. Writing words that sound the same, room, spoon, noon, etc.
4. Cutting out and labelling pictures.
5. Preparing lists of words related to touch, smell, sound, feeling, e.g. touch: soft, hard, rough, smooth, sticky, damp, icy, wet, etc.
6. Preparing recipes, shopping lists, etc.
7. String words: The teacher says or writes a sentence like this: I went to town and I bought apples; then he asks individual students to say the sentence with an additional word each time. e.g. I went to town and I bought apples and bread. I went to town and I bought apples, bread and coffee, and so on. The game can be played alphabetically.
8. Crossword puzzles.

5.12

Vocabulary Tests

Tests are necessary to see how pupils are progressing and to check their grasp of lexical items. A good teacher is always assessing his students' progress either through formal tests or informally by the routine questions he asks in the classroom. In addition, testing vocabulary motivates students to study. It also supplies information. However, vocabulary tests should be valid and reliable to meet these objectives.

The teacher, when designing a vocabulary test, should be aware of what he is going to test, whether he is after understanding words, meanings or producing other synonyms, or both comprehension and production of words. Also the teacher should not make the instructions or the wording of questions difficult or tricky so that students can understand quite clearly what is required, and what is going to be tested.

[1] This game is from *English Teaching Forum*, Vol. 19/2, 1981.

Vocabulary tests are numerous and of different levels and aims. However, the most common ones that are often employed by foreign language teachers are:

1. Words and their connotations; e.g.:
   Sculpture: statue, stone, visage, pedestal, etc.

2. Words and their opposites – antonyms; e.g.:
   She tried to *conceal* her feelings, but her eyes _____ the truth. (reveal)

3. Fill in spaces (from a list or without), e.g.:
   The recent earthquake in Turkey has left thousands of people starving and _____ (homeless)

4. Complete sentences from options; e.g.:
   Do you (fill, feel, fall, fell) better today?

5. A variation of this type of question is the following:
   I asked him to mention the main points on the _____ for the next meeting.
   (a) memory   (b) diary   (c) agenda   (d) discussion (Answer: agenda)

6. Synonyms – choose the word or phrase that has the same meaning as the underlined word, e.g.:
   The play was disappointing to the audience but it was <u>highly appreciated</u> by many critics.
       (a) easily rejected   (b) violently attacked
       (c) simply greeted   (d) strongly applauded

7. Word formation; e.g.: He *intends* to become a doctor. Do you know what his _____ are? (intentions)
   Another type of word formation is spelling of combinations, e.g.: happy + ness = happiness

8. Definitions; e.g. use one word instead of the underlined words. The first two letters are given to you:
   Before going to England, a student is advised to find a suitable furnished <u>room to live in</u> beforehand.   ac . . . (accommodation)

9. Words and idioms: Choose the answer which best describes the underlined idiom:
   The problem with the pay talks is that they have reached a <u>stalemate</u>.
       (a) final stage   (b) an expected settlement
       (c) fierce fight   (d) a situation where no solution is possible

10. Odd-man-out; e.g.
    table, chair, book, sofa, bed (*Book* because it is not furniture)

11. Matching. This can be either adjectives with nouns, e.g. premeditated murder, voluntary retirement, etc., or nouns with verbs; buy souvenir, discuss topic, etc.

12. Cloze test. In such tests, a passage is taken and words are deleted from it at regular intervals. The teacher can modify the test by supplying the first letter of each missing word or by deleting one class of words (nouns, verbs, prepositions, etc.), or by providing a list of the target words.
    There are other types of vocabulary tests. The teacher should refer to books dealing with language testing for further exercises and drills.

Chapter Six

Teaching Grammar

Introduction

The concept of 'grammar' is viewed differently by the various schools of linguists. According to the traditionalists it is a collection of rules and principles; while to the structuralists, it is the study of how sentences are arranged and formed. The transformationalists consider it as the rules that generate infinite sentences and allow speakers to understand utterances they have never heard of; whereas to some exponents of the communicative approach, it is the functions and notions of language as opposed to structural patterns. Whatever concept is utilized, grammar remains the internal organization of the language. A language cannot be learned without learning its grammar because it is the element that makes meaning in language use.

The issue with grammar is not whether or not it should be learned, but rather how it can be presented to learners. This chapter thus aims at developing a knowledge of grammar for use. Pupils should understand and produce linguistic forms as part of a purposeful activity, not just as an exercise in language practice.

These linguistic forms which are referred to as 'grammar' involve language morphology and syntax. The former shows the changes in word form resulting either from inflections (such as plurality, verb tense, aspects, possession, etc.) or from derivations as in prefixes or suffixes. On the other hand, syntax deals with word order and how words combine to make sentences.

The following sections focus on communicative grammar, which combines simultaneously a knowledge of linguistic rules and performance. The structuralists' view of grammar will also be discussed, since it is more systematic and can easily describe any utterance in precise terms. Also, notional grammar will not be presented in detail because there is no grammar book available which reflects completely a functional/notional approach.

6.1

Grammar Theories

There are different theories of grammar affecting English teaching methodology. The FL teacher should consult linguistic reference books in order to acquire more information about the subject. This section will deal briefly with the theories and their relation to foreign language learning.

Traditional Grammar

This aspect of grammar is based on classical and inflected languages such as Greek and Latin. Traditional grammarians established eight parts of speech due to the influence of Latin; noun, pronoun, adjective, verb, adverb, preposition, conjunction and interjection. They defined these parts by their meanings or functions. Thus, a noun is 'the name of a person, place, thing, quality or abstract entity', or an adverb is 'a word which modifies a verb or another adverb'. Such definitions are sometimes confusing. For example, in the sentence 'He runs home', the word 'home' functions both as noun and adverb because it signals the name of a place and modifies the verb 'runs' simultaneously.

In addition, traditional grammarians categorize words within sentences as subject, object, verb, direct object, indirect object, complement, and so on. They also list nouns according to cases, namely: nominative, vocative, accusative, genitive, dative and instrumental. Examples: knife, O knife! knife, of the knife, to the knife and with the knife. Furthermore, traditional grammarians prescribe certain rules about how people ought to speak or write the language. These definitions do not help the foreign language learner to understand the target language satisfactorily.

Nevertheless, the contribution of traditional grammar to foreign language learning is considerable. Thus, along with its practical definitions of the parts of speech, it also gives useful definitions of basic structures such as phrases, clauses and sentences. Furthermore, it provides the teacher with simple 'rules' to teach the language. Probably for these reasons, traditional grammar is still used in one form or another in foreign language classes.

Structural Grammar

This type of grammar is descriptive. It postulates that language has a set of grammatical patterns in which words are arranged to convey meaning which is determined by word form, function words, word order and intonation patterns such as stress, pitch and juncture. Moreover, structural linguists classify the parts of speech according to form and according to function, i.e. syntactic position. Class words involve nouns, verbs, adjectives and adverbs. They carry the basic lexical meaning and inflect to mark meaning; e.g. boy – boys, do – does – did – done, happy – happiness – happily, great – greatness – greater, etc.

However, such a definition has its own limitations. Not all nouns ending in s are plurals (e.g. Chaos, loneliness) and not all nouns take s in the plural (e.g. sheep, deer). Also, not all adjectives make the comparative in (-er), nor do all adverbs end in (-ly) as in fast and hard which function as different parts of speech with no change in form.

Defining words by form is impossible, and the part of speech of a word varies according to its function in a sentence. When analysing parts of speech, close attention should be paid to grammatical signals and to word order in addition to inflectional and derivational suffixes. Considering words in isolation is not an indication of their grammatical function; as they should be seen in the perspective of phrases and sentences.

Descriptive grammarians have extensively studied the question of the structure of sentences and their constituents of lexical or functional forms.

They have developed several strategies for this purpose such as immediate constituent analysis, often called IC grammar. Another is phrase structure grammar which involves systemic grammar (Halliday). In addition, there are tagmemic grammar (Pike and Fries) and stratificational grammar.[1] All these varieties of structural grammars of English are concerned with language performance – spoken or written – and not with competence. They also assume that the construction of English sentences has two parts. Each part can be divided into further words. Such analytical description is usually done according to certain frames like the binary division or the phrase structure tree as shown in the following examples:

	Sentence proper (SP)					Sentence modifier (SM)
1	The little girl	ate	two apples			yesterday
	NP	VP				
2	The little girl	ate	two apples			yesterday
	D NP	V	NP			
3	The little girl	ate	two apples			yesterday
	ADJ N		ADJ N			
4	The little girl	ate	two apples			yesterday

On the phrase-structure tree, the analysis of the sentence will be like this:

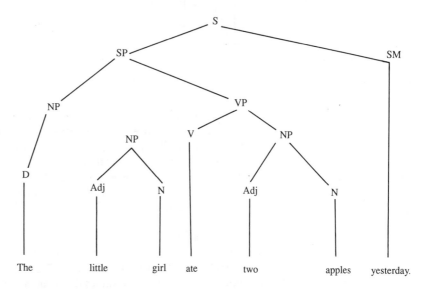

The abbreviations used are:
S = sentence, SP = sentence proper, SM = sentence modifier, NP = noun phrase, VP = verb phrase, D = determiner, Adj = adjective

[1] Foreign language teachers and learners should consult linguistic reference books for more details about types of structural grammars of English, since these are beyond the scope of this book.

A variation of the phrase-structure tree is the tree-diagram in which the specified nodes are not directly relevant to the sentence under discussion. Instead, they are used to show where branching occurs, and where additional elements could be inserted. The higher ones represent basic relationships essential to sentence building or to manifest the surface structure of the sentence. However, the use of this technique is limited and often used in the transformational-generative grammar. The above sentence 'The little girl ate two apples yesterday' can be analysed, according to 'tree diagram technique', as follows:

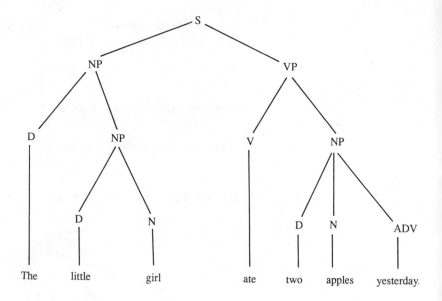

The teacher may utilize such analytical description to demonstrate how the part of speech of a word is determined by the slot it fills or the function it performs in the sentence and how this function is controlled by the grammatical signals associated with it.

This system of analysis is also helpful in teaching different structural points or morphological variations as we can substitute any item or element in the sentence as required.

Transformational Grammar

Transformational Grammar (TG), often called generative grammar, was pioneered by Noam Chomsky in 1957. It was subsequently modified by other linguists. This theory assumes that language is based on a system of rules, and not on a set of speech habits as the structuralists maintain. These 'phrase structure rules' are capable of producing an infinite number of meaningful sentences at the level of surface structure. This is done through a process of transformations such as substitutions, re-arrangement, addition, deletion and combinations. The basic sentence types as described by Roberts (1962), are:

(a) N + V

Birds fly, or

N + V + adv.

She speaks softly, or

D + N + V + adv.

The girl sings merrily.

(b) D + N + V + adj.

The teacher seems happy.

(c) D + N + V + D + N

The student became a teacher.

(d) D + N + V + D + N

The baby ate an apple, or

N + V + N

Girls play basketball.

(e) D + N + V + D + N + D + N

The teacher gave his pupils a test, or

N + V + N + D + N

They wrote him a letter.

(f) N + V + N + D + N

They considered him a hero, or

D + N + V + D + N + adj.

The children think their parents great, or

N + V + D + N + adj.

They painted their house white.

(g) N + V + N + N

They elected her chairman, or

D + N + V + N + N

The committee appointed him secretary.

(h) N + be + adv.

She is here, or

N + be + P + D + N

She is in the house.

(i) D + N + be + adj.

The teacher is absent.

(j) N + be + D + N

He is an officer.

These basic sentences can produce an infinite variety of meaningful sentences with the help of certain transformation operations. For example:

(a) 'There' transformations, e.g.

A book is on the table   – There is a book on the table

(b) Question transformations, e.g.:

The boys play there.   – Who plays there?

The boys play there.   – Where do the boys play?

The boys played yesterday.   – When did the boys play? etc.

(c) Passive transformations, e.g.:

The boy broke the window.	– The window was broken.
She is making tea.	– Tea is being made by her.

(d) Miscellaneous transformations, e.g.:

The student is clever.	– It is the student who is clever.
The student is clever.	– It is necessary for a student to be clever.

The student is clever. ⎫
The clever student. ⎬ Ali is a clever student.
Ali is a student. ⎭

In addition, generative grammar introduces meaning as an integral part of any grammatical study. It also offers a basis for explaining the ambiguity of certain sentences like: Flying planes can be dangerous, or, visiting relatives can be tiresome. Nevertheless, this type of grammar is not commonly used in English classes at the secondary-school level. This grammar uses symbols, numbers, abbreviations and formula-like description which make it too difficult for pupils to understand.

Grammar and the Communicative Approach

Communicatively-taught grammar is a modern linguistic approach that emerged in the late 1970s as a reaction against prevalent structural grammar. It was established by British linguists, namely Wilkins, Hymes, Candlin, Widdowson and others. This approach tries to reconcile language usage with use. That is, to acquire grammar not simply as linguistic forms (e.g., present perfect, present progressive, past tense, phrasal verbs, relatives, etc.), but also as a communicative resource. While the structural technique concentrates largely on the form of the items, communicatively-taught grammar gives prominence to the meaning of the grammatical forms as specified by the functional tags. The main characteristics of this treatment of grammar can be summed up as follows:

(a) It involves the use of form and meaning of language items simultaneously. It takes into consideration knowledge of linguistic rules, that is rules of the construction of the language, and the ability to manipulate this knowledge for communicative purposes. Grammatical forms, therefore, are taught not for their own sake as in structural or traditional grammar, but as a means of carrying out communicative acts.

However, this approach does not focus on the grammatical form of items, nor does it give abstract descriptions or definitions. Instead, it concentrates on the meanings or the notions underlying these forms. This is followed lest the communicative aspect of the language be lost in the effort of mastering the grammatical form through conventional practice or manipulation of sentences. The main purpose is to help the learners build up language competence through use, and not through knowledge of linguistic rules.

(b) Through its emphasis on meaning, this approach assumes that incorrect grammatical forms (e.g. I have speak, She go everyday to school, etc.) can be eradicated gradually as the learner advances in learning and in using the language. Confusion in the conceptual meaning (i.e. of grammatical notions) is more difficult to overcome in later stages. Hence, notions and functions should coexist with structures. The learner should know first *which* notions or ideas he wants to communicate. Subsequently he expresses these notions or concepts through communicative functions, i.e. speech acts encoded into grammatical forms.

(c) It tries to express the various notions or meanings that may belong to a single grammatical form as it introduces them separately and in different situations or stages in order to highlight their meaning and use. The meanings of verb tenses and modals are good examples of this grammar. For example, the different grammatical notions of the modal 'will', namely: willingness, polite requests, intention, insistence and prediction can best be taught at different stages since the situations in which these notions are used differ greatly. This strategy of presenting one notion at a time ensures that all possible notions are introduced as separate teaching objectives.

(d) Another feature of this approach is connected with the process of learning. It is less teacher centred. The communicative activities associated with it make pupils less dependent on the teacher as the giver of knowledge. Pupils are encouraged to recognize for themselves grammatical forms as they are working out activities in groups, pairs or individually.

Despite all these merits, the communicative teaching of grammar suffers from the following shortcomings:

(a) To teach linguistic forms and language functions together as linked pairs might confuse pupils and might lead them to overgeneralize or draw wrong conclusions. Thus they may believe that each linguistic form can only express one particular function.

(b) Too much emphasis on functional meaning would not give pupils sufficient knowledge of the linguistic rules (i.e. system of the language) to carry out or extend a communicative task efficiently. A structural/notional grammar would be more appropriate to avoid the danger of focusing on form or meaning.

(c) To many teachers, communicatively-taught grammar does not seem systematic or coherent as it is restricted to the notions and functions of the language. This usually occurs randomly rather than logically. Consequently this grammar is not clearly defined or expressed through a convenient system because grammatical forms are encoded into communicative functions.

(d) Grammar taught in this way requires a competent teacher, so that he can create appropriate communicative situations to provide the pupils with the opportunity to practise the grammar points in a natural interesting way, and not through the manipulation of linguistic exercises or sentences. Such an EFL teacher is difficult to find in a foreign context where all FL teachers are non-native speakers of the target language.

6.2

Grammatical Meaning

Recognition of the function of each element is essential for comprehending an utterance, as each word, phrase or notion in it plays a certain role in conveying its message. Content words, in the first place, provide us with the lexical meaning (i.e. dictionary meaning) which is basic in understanding the general meaning of the sentence. On the other hand, grammatical meaning is determined by word order within the sentence, (inflection, structure words, syntax), concord or arrangement, and intonation and stress. These components will be discussed with some detail in the following sections.

Inflections

These are of two types: inflectional suffixes and derivational affixes. The former refers to a change in the form of a word to show different syntactical relationships. The latter refers to word formation where new words are formed by the addition of prefixes or suffixes or both. Inflectional suffixes are limited in number and do not change the part of speech of a word. They can be classified as follows:

(a) *Plural of nouns.* This form has several varieties as follows:

Singular	Plural	Phonetic transcript	Suffix
cat	cats	/kæts/	_____s
ball	balls	/bɔːlz/	_____z
dish	dishes	/dɪʃɪz/	_____iz
wife	wives	/waivz/	_____vz
ox	oxen	/oksən/	_____en

(b) *The possessive of nouns:* The ('s) that forms the possessive of nouns in English follows the same pattern /s/, /z/ and /iz/ that conditions the plural form. Examples:

/s/	/z/	/iz/
Jack's	Fred's	Rose's
/dʒks/	/fredz/	/rəʊzɪz/

(c) *The third person singular present tense of verbs:* The s-ending that occurs in the third person singular of the simple present tense follows also the same pattern that conditions the plural morpheme. Examples:

/s/	/z/	/ɪz/
eats	sees	dresses
/iːts/	/siːz/	/dresɪz/

(d) *The past-tense form:* The markers of the past form of regular verbs are /t/, /d/, or /ɪd/, while irregular formations of the past tense and of the past participle have different inflectional endings. Examples:

	/t/	/d/	/ɪd/
Regular	lick/licked	rub/rubbed	want/wanted
verbs	/lɪkt/	/rʌbd/	/wɒntɪd/
Irregular	write	wrote	written
verbs	/rait/	/rəʊt/	/rɪtn/
	sleep	slept	slept
	/sliːp/	/slept/	/slept/

(e) *The progressive form:* The suffix (-ing) is used with the helping verb (be) to form the continuous tense. Example: Ali is playing football. It may substitute for an adjective e.g.: Cats are fascinating creatures; or it may function as a gerund, e.g.: Swimming is a good exercise.

(f) *The past participle form:* The (ed) ending is added to the verb to form the past participle with its perfective and passive functions. Example: has written, was cleaned.

(g) *The comparative and superlative markers (er) and (est):* These occur with adjectives and are also inflectional suffixes. Examples: taller, tallest.

Derivational affixes, on the other hand, are numerous and mark a change in the word class: noun to verb, verb to noun, noun to adjective, adjective to adverb and so on. This device of word formation is an effective means of increasing vocabulary and of identifying the functional use of a word. Some common suffixes and their use are:

suffix	signal	example
-ize	verb	realize
-tion	noun	preparation
-en	verb	shorten

The following list illustrates some of the most common affixes:

1.

verb	adjective	noun
act	active	activity/actor
describe	descriptive	description
depend	dependent	dependence

2.

noun	verb	adjective
shortness	shorten	short
courage	encourage	courageous
horror	horrify	horrible
form	formalize	formal

3.

adjective	noun	verb
real	realization	realize
simple	simplification	simplify
dark	darkness	darken
clear	clarity	clarify

4.

verb	noun	adjective
amuse	amusement	amusing
accept	acceptance	acceptable
like	likeness	likely

5.

noun	adjective	adverb
fortune	fortunate	fortunately
happiness	happy	happily
kindness	kind	kindly

Structure Words

Structure (or function) words like: the, can, do, to, of, but, because, when, who, and, that add to the content words some clarification and some grammatical relationships that are essential to the meaning of the utterance.

They constitute the framework on which content words like girl, write, friend, etc. are fixed.[1]

Syntax – Word Order

Syntax (i.e. how sentences are structured) is an important source of meaning since the order in which the words are put determines the function they have in the sentence. Consequently changes in the order of words often result in differences in grammatical function as well as in the meaning of the utterance. For example:

1. You saw the teacher.
   The teacher saw you.
2. The armchair is damaged.
   The chair arm is damaged.
3. Only the teacher came.
   The only teacher came.
4. She has written a letter.
   Has she written a letter?
5. She wrote a letter to her friend.
   She wrote her friend a letter.
6. Had she studied well, she would have passed the exam.
   If she had studied well, she would have passed the exam.

Each pair of the first four examples has sentences containing identical lexical items. However, each sentence has a different meaning because of the order of words in the sentence. For example, in: You saw the teacher/The teacher saw you, the lexical units are the same in both sentences. Yet their meanings are quite different since 'You' in the first sentence functions as the performer of the action, whereas it is the receiver of the action in the second.

Another variation of syntax is the normal sequence of sentence structure. For example, a combination like 'boy the on put table book' does not make any sense, although we know the lexical meaning of each word. This is because the words do not have syntactical structure. The whole collection is, therefore, nonsense.

Concord or Agreement[2]

This grammatical device indicates agreement of words in a sentence. There are several types of concord, but the most important one in English is concord of number between subject and verb. For example, there is agreement of subject and verb. Here are some examples:

1. He/She drinks milk every day.
2. I/We/You/They drink milk every day.
3. The pen is lost. The pens are lost.
   The man is present. The men are present.
4. How they got there does not concern me.
5. That she can come is good news.

Other variations of subject–verb agreement are notional concord and

[1] See Chapter 6 on Teaching Vocabulary where structure words are discussed.
[2] The teacher should consult grammar reference books for more details on this topic.

proximity. The former is concord according to the idea of number – singular or plural. For example: The audience are enjoying the play (every one in the group).

The audience is enjoying the play (the group as one entity).

Proximity, on the other hand, indicates agreement of the verb with the nearest noun or pronoun that immediately precedes it. Examples:

– No one except the girls reject his offer.
– Either the pupils or the teacher supports this opinion.

Concord of persons follows this principle of proximity. Example:
Neither you, nor I, nor the teacher knows the answer.

Other types of concord are also indicated in the following grammatical forms:

(a) Singular and plural forms of demonstrative adjectives. Examples:
   – This boy   These boys   That car   Those cars.
(b) Subject-complement concord of numbers. Examples:
   – The man is a doctor.   The men are doctors.
   – A dog is an animal.   Dogs are animals.
(c) Subject–object concord of number, person, and gender. Examples:
   – She injured herself in the accident.
   – They wrote their tasks, etc.

6.3 Notion/Function vs. Pattern/Sentence

These four concepts are sometimes misunderstood by foreign language learners. Notions and functions, in the first place, are both a way of describing language from a semantic point of view. Notional meaning is, however, conceptual such as notions of time, space, location, quantity, case. On the other hand, functional meaning is social such as functions of agreement, approving, forgiving, inferring, greeting, etc. Notions are concepts (i.e. ideas) underlying functions (i.e. speech acts). In other words, notions are expressed through communicative functions which are in turn, encoded through several language forms or exponents. This process may be represented diagrammatically as follows:

Situation→notion→function→form

This is the main concern of the communicative syllabus in which the grammatical forms are approached through meaning (i.e. through notions and functions).

Patterns and sentences, however, are a way of describing language from a formal point of view. Nevertheless, the pattern is the underlying design or formula of a sentence which functions as an actual utterance like a communicative function. Patterns, in this respect, may be equated with notions. Sentences can also be equated to functions since both are encoded through grammatical forms. However, the approach with structural grammar is different as shown below:

Situation→form/pattern→sentence→meaning.

This way of approaching meaning through form is the cornerstone of structural grammar which is still followed in our schools.

Patterns in English are limited in number. There are only eight basic patterns in the language, and for each one there is an infinite number of utterances based on it. These major patterns are the following:

1. S + V   adv.   e.g.   Mariam is in the house.
2. S + V   e.g.   The child laughed.
3. S + V + O   e.g.   Somebody caught the ball.
4. S + V + Cs   e.g.   Fatima is kind.
5. S + V + O + Co   e.g.   We have proved him wrong.
6. S + V + O$_1$ + O$_2$ e.g.   She sent him a letter.
7. S + V + O + adv e.g.   He put the plate on the table.
8. There + be + noun + adverb. e.g. There is a dog in the garden.[1]

The above sentences are condensed examples of the basic patterns. They can be expanded by adding new elements or forms to each of them. Thus, the sentence of the second pattern (S + V) can be extended into a sentence like: 'The young child laughed merrily', and similarly with the other sentences.

6.4

Design of a Grammar Lesson

For presenting and practising the new structure, the teacher may attempt the following procedures:

Step 1: Presentation of new structure.
Step 2: Identification of the new structure.
Step 3: Drills and practice, mechanical or manipulative drills.
Step 4: Meaningful drills.
Step 5: Communicative drills.

Step 1: Presentation of new structure

1. Evoke the new structure by reminding pupils of a familiar dialogue, or text, in which it was used.

2. Use the new structure in a simple dialogue or conversation whose words and forms are familiar to pupils. Another possibility is to accompany the new structure with actions to illustrate its meaning. For example, in demonstrating the regular past tense, the teacher may say, while acting, 'I am cleaning the chalkboard'. He stops, turns to the class and says 'I have cleaned the chalkboard', and so on.

3. Repeat the new pattern several times; then have it repeated, in chorus, by appropriate groups. After that ask individual pupils to repeat it. It is a good idea to start with more able pupils so that the less able ones may have more time to listen to and repeat reasonably correct sentences.

4. For those grammatical structures which are difficult to present in a context, the teacher may present the rule or give a formal explanation as long as it is supplemented by sufficient examples and practice.

5. It is more effective and more motivating to give examples related to the pupils' experience. In this regard the teacher is advised to use the names of the pupils in his sentences and attach to those names actions, habits, behaviour, facts and so on.

[1] S = subject, V = verb, adv. = adverb, O = object, O$_1$ = direct object, O$_2$ = indirect object, Cs = subject complement, Co = object complement.

Step 2: Identification of the new pattern

After oral presentation, the teacher writes the new pattern on the blackboard for further discussion. Thus he may draw the pupils' attention to the form of that pattern: word order, concord, inversion, inflections, spelling, function words, punctuation, etc. If necessary, he can give more examples to reinforce the pupils' comprehension of both meaning or form. He may also ask them questions that lead to the use of the new pattern in order to check their understanding of its function or structure.

Step 3: Mechanical drills

Once the structure has been presented, the teacher gives the class some manipulative drills. The purpose of such drills is to help pupils learn the forms of the new pattern and to practise oral fluency. They are usually conducted chorally and by means of a tape-recorder. The students repeat after the model following a technique, usually called four-phased drill.[1]

As soon as the pupils have learned the pattern, mechanical drills should be abandoned so as to avoid boredom in the classroom.

The following are some of the possible manipulative drill types:

Repetition drills

The teacher simply provides the model containing the new structure and the pupils repeat it. The class responds as a whole chorally, then as groups and finally individually.

Substitution drills

These drills vary according to the position of the words to be substituted and the number of cues. Most effective ones are simple and multiple substitution.

Simple substitution: This is often called substitution with one cue. In this drill the pupils are given a sentence and a cue word. They are to substitute the cue words in their appropriate place in the sentence. A noun is replaced by a noun, a verb by another verb, an adjective by another adjective and so on. Examples:

1. I go to the supermarket every day. (every week)
2. I go to the supermarket every week. (every month)
3. I go to the supermarket every month. (every Friday)
4. I go to the supermarket every Friday. (she)
5. She goes to the supermarket every day. (beach)
6. She goes to the beach every day. (school)
7. She goes to the school every day, and so on.

Multiple substitution: In this drill the basic sentence remains the same but the cue could be a substitute for any item in the model. Suppose the model sentence is 'I wrote a good book' the drill will progress in this way:

Teacher	:	Ali
Pupil	:	Ali wrote a good book.
Teacher	:	story

[1] Four-phased drill is a variation of repetition drill. It is used widely in the initial stages of learning English. The technique is conducted in the following manner: (1) The teacher gives the stimulus; (2) A pupil responds to the teacher's stimulus; (3) The teacher repeats the correct response; (4) The whole class repeats after the teacher.

Pupil	:	Ali wrote a good story.
Teacher	:	love
Pupil	:	Ali wrote a love story.
Teacher	:	bought
Pupil	:	Ali bought a love story.
Teacher	:	two
Pupil	:	Ali bought two love stories.

It is essential, when conducting such drills, for pupils to be attentive so that they can remember what is said in each sentence in order to form the new one.

Chain drill

In this drill all pupils have the chance to ask and answer a question in a chain-like manner. The drill goes as follows:

Teacher	:	My name is Ali What is your name?
Pupil 1	:	My name is Sameer. What is your name?
Pupil 2	:	My name is Ahmad What is your name? etc.

The teacher may conduct this type of drill in this way:

Teacher	:	I see the map, Ali, do you see it?
Ali	:	Yes, I see it. I see the tree, Jasim, do you see it!
Jasim	:	Yes, I see it. I see the car, Ahmad, do you see it?
Ahmad	:	Yes, I see it, etc.

Transformation

In this drill the pupils are given a sentence to transform into another – e.g. a question, or a negative or a passive sentence. Examples:

Teacher	:	I go to the store every day.
Pupil	:	I do not go to the store every day.
Teacher	:	I go to the cinema every week.
Pupil	:	Do you go to the cinema every week? and so on.

Expansion drill

In this drill the pupils are given a word or expression to be added to the model sentence. Example:

Teacher	:	I have a pen (always)
Pupil	:	I always have a pen.
Teacher	:	I see a girl (with red hair).
Pupil	:	I see a girl with red hair.

Integrative drill

In this type of drill, the teacher presents two short sentences and asks pupils to combine them into one. Examples:

1. I have a pencil. It's red.
   I have a red pencil.
2. The man is in the store. He is my father.
   The man in the store is my father.
3. I went to the store. Ali went to the store.
   I went to the store and Ali did too, etc.

Step 4: Meaningful drills

With mechanical drills the emphasis is on form and on automaticity, and there is only one response to the stimulus predetermined by the teacher. Conversely, meaningful drills focus on content instead of form, and the response can be expressed in more than one way. Yet the teacher knows in advance what the pupil ought to answer as meaningful drills are controlled by the teacher. Some examples are:

Restatement

To conduct this drill, the teacher whispers to a pupil to ask another pupil a question. The second pupil is instructed to answer. Example:

Teacher	:	(whispering) Sabah, ask Muna what she did yesterday.
Sabah	:	Muna, what did you do yesterday?
Muna	:	I visited my friend, Layla, etc.

This drill can be conducted as 'chain drills'. The pupils carry on the drill by themselves without being given the cues by the teacher as in manipulative drills. In the above example, Muna would turn to the pupil sitting beside her and ask the question she had just answered, and so on.

Rejoinder

The teacher makes a statement containing a certain syntactic structure, then a pupil responds by communicating something about himself. For example:

Teacher	:	I like to study.
Pupil	:	You like to study, but I don't.
Teacher	:	I don't play football.
Pupil	:	You don't play football and I don't either.

Question and answer

The teacher poses a question; one pupil responds with a free choice of answer. Instead of the teacher asking, pairs of pupils question each other in chain fashion – Examples:

Teacher	:	What's your hobby?
Pupil	:	My hobby is collecting stamps.
Teacher	:	What is your favourite lesson?
Pupil	:	English is my favourite lesson.

Situation drills

These are the most commonly used drills in the classroom setting because of their practicality and applicability. A situation drill can be used to show the meaning of a structure or to distinguish two structures that have similar meanings through actions, drawings, objects and other illustrations. In fact, there are several techniques that can make structural drills meaningful and consequently interesting. However, before reviewing these techniques and procedures of contextualization, the teacher is advised to observe the following points so as to make situational practice more effective:

(a) The sentences containing the structural item that is being taught should be simple, relatively short and relevant to the pupils' experience.

(b) There must be some cohesion between the chosen sentences. That is, they should be in a series (i.e. in a sequence) and related to one idea so as to be easy to dramatize or to repeat.

(c) The situation used should be obvious and capable of admitting only one interpretation or response in order to avoid confusion.

The following are a few of the techniques that are employed.

1. *Use of charts, drawings, pictures, filmstrips, transparencies, objects or actions:* These visual devices can be particularly useful in the early stages of learning English and with young children. However, they can also be utilized at the secondary school level if they are sufficiently sophisticated. Examples include the following:

Example I: Look at the chart and answer the questions:

Teacher : Is it a bus? (Referring to picture No. 1)
Pupil   : Yes, it is. It's a bus.

Teacher : Is it a bicycle? (Referring to picture No. 2)
Pupil   : Yes, it is. It's a bicycle.

Example II: Look at the chart. Make sentences as in the examples:

Teacher : The girl
Pupil   : The girl is writing. She's writing a letter.

Teacher : The boys
Pupil   : The boys are playing. They're playing football.

2. *Use of dialogue or situations:* These devices are common techniques and are popular with both teachers and pupils. The pupils first listen to a dialogue, then they practise in several ways. Thus, they may repeat each sentence, or take the part of the speakers until the dialogue or situation is thoroughly grasped. The teacher may select from it certain patterns to be practised by the class in the form of drills which may be purely mechanical or of a question-and-answer type. Stress and intonation should be kept the same as in real conversations. Examples of one situation for the whole drill:

– Do you want an orange?
– Well, I like oranges, but I don't want one now. Thank you, etc.
– Do you want some tea?
– Well, I like tea, but I don't want any now. Thank you, etc.

3. *Factual drills:* These are mainly of the question-and-answer type. In such drills the teacher must always make sure that the pupils are practising the natural responses. He may provide them with names, or ask about objects familiar to the pupils. Examples:

(a) Teacher : Where did you go yesterday?
    Pupil A : I went to the zoo.
    Teacher : What did he say?
    Pupil B : He said he went to the zoo.
(b) Teacher : How often does Ali visit you?
    Pupil   : He visits me almost every week.
    Teacher : When did he visit you last?
    Pupil   : He last visited me yesterday, etc.

Step 5: Communicative drills

Once the teacher feels that the pupils have grasped the new structure, either in isolation or after practising mechanical or meaningful drills, he gives them some communicative practice using the new structure in context.

In communicative drills there is no control of the response. The pupils are free to express themselves or their ideas. However, the teacher has to instruct them to respond truthfully and to make them feel that what they contribute is of significance to the others. The following interaction activities are typical:

Interviews: The aim is to practise fluency in question and answer situations. There are different types of interview assignments. One involves bringing a pupil to the front of the class to be interviewed by another pupil who may ask him about his hobbies, family life, opinions on a particular issue, why he did certain things, etc.

The activity can be played as a press conference with several pupils acting as reporters asking the 'minister', 'visitor', 'film star', etc., questions about current events or world affairs.

The activity can also be presented in the classroom as 'applying for a job'. The class interviews several pupils to fill an imaginary vacancy. The class then confers to decide which applicant is best qualified for the job.

The game can take the form of questioning the teacher. Each pupil prepares questions to ask the teacher, who answers them in the next lesson.

As a variation of the above, the teacher pairs the pupils off to interview each other about a particular topic. While interviewing, pupils take notes and collect data with a view to using them to write biographical sketches as practice of creative writing.

Role-playing: This is another technique which affords an opportunity to practise a new structure in the context of natural communicative usage. In this activity a situation is presented to a small group of pupils who may act it out. For example, the teacher can suggest that the pupils pair off and role-play the parts of newspaper reporters or of taking/giving an order in a restaurant, greeting people formally or informally, etc. A list of useful words and expressions could be given to the groups.

Problem-solving: In this activity the pupils are given a problem that requires a solution achieved through small group discussions. The value of such activities is to allow pupils to use new structures and vocabulary in a natural context. Before conducting the activity, the teacher has to present the necessary vocabulary that the class will need to employ.

While conducting communicative activities, the teacher must not keep interrupting the flow of the activity to correct pupils' utterances as this might inhibit them from further participation. He should also not reject pupils' contributions as being ungrammatical. Errors are inevitable; therefore, they should be seen as a normal part of the process of acquiring the target language.

Although correction of errors is a major part of language teaching, the teacher has to postpone this until the activity is over. He then revises with the class the correct rules of English grammar and use.

6.5

Correcting Mistakes in Drilling

There are two main purposes in conducting drills. One is to explain the meaning of a structural point by presenting it in a natural context. The pupils can thus use it properly when it is encountered in everyday communication. If structures are taught only by stating rules and giving examples, many of them may seem unreal. Therefore, the drills should be simple, realistic and lend themselves to dramatization. Only in this way can pupils appreciate and enjoy practising such drills.

The other aim is to minimize the role of the teacher in the classroom by making pupils practise the language themselves. However, there are occasions or situations where the intervention of the teacher is necessary. This usually happens with purely manipulative or meaningful drills which are dependent upon the teacher's direction for a response. But with communicative drills the teacher's control is relinquished because the pupils themselves determine the response.

Consequently, the teacher's corrections must be undertaken selectively but according to the type of the drill. Thus, in mechanical drills where the objective is to internalize new structures, the teacher is advised to correct the mistake as soon as it occurs. This immediate correction is necessary because the objective of a manipulative drill is mainly to acquire linguistic competence and to make pupils utter the sentences with normal automaticity. However, repeated correction of pronunciation errors distracts pupils' attention from the structural point of the drill.

At the meaningful drill stage, pupils usually concentrate on content rather than form. That is, on the answer which is true in content rather than correct in form; and pupils' mistakes are more likely to be performance errors. The pupils, at this stage, are assumed to know the structures of the language but they may be unable to express their ideas properly. Here the teacher can draw the attention of pupils to the mistake in order to allow them to correct it themselves, or he may give them the appropriate form of expression. Because meaningful drills are somewhat manipulative, the teacher is advised to insist on correct responses in terms of both form and content.

Finally, in communication drills, pupils are free to say whatever they want. The emphasis here is on the message and on what they say rather than on how they say it. The teacher, therefore, should overlook mistakes, except for serious errors, in order not to inhibit pupils from participating effectively in the activity.

Chapter Seven

Teaching
Cultural Features

Introduction

The preceding three chapters have discussed the subsystems of the English language, namely sounds, vocabulary and grammar. Some procedures for their teaching were also suggested. However, the learning of these linguistic elements is inadequate for the acquisition of communicative competence unless we know their appropriate use within each situation. That is, when to use them and under what circumstances they are appropriate. This social use of the language involves, among other things, cultural allusions or conventions such as ways of thinking, custom, mores, art forms, idioms, etc. It also involves paralinguistic features like tone of voice, gestures and facial expression. Such cultural features are essential to understand the ideas and meanings entailed in speech acts. For example, a foreign language learner should comprehend references or expressions that often occur in the written or spoken language such as: 'He's as old as the hills', 'pretty as a picture', or proverbs like: 'more haste, less speed', etc. The learner must also be able to interpret the figurative use of language, e.g. 'He's the lord of the road', 'Fair as a star when only one is shining in the sky', or expressions like 'the bar' for lawyers collectively, etc. He must also conform to norms of English culture, knowing which expressions are polite, acceptable, formal, informal, etc., both in speaking and writing. In addition, he needs to understand nonverbal communication such as nods, smiles and the like.

The ignorance of such cultural features would create misunderstanding between a listener and a speaker, or a writer and a reader. In terms of foreign language learning, this situation (i.e. being unaware of cultural content) indicates incapacity to use the language appropriately. Hence gaining cultural knowledge of the target language is an integral part of the learning process. The following sections deal with the role of culture in foreign language learning.

7.1

Culture and Foreign Language Learning

There is a close relationship between language and culture. The former is both a product and a reflection of the latter. What the people of a particular culture talk and think is shaped and communicated in the vocabulary of the language they use. Thus, learning a second language involves the learning of the culture of the people who speak it, because these two aspects are intimately bound together. This can be illustrated by citing some of the cultural differences between English and Arabic:

(a) Family environment including size and marriage, etc. Examples: An Arab family is characterized by its relatively large size, strong relationships between its members, parental care, intricate traditions of marriage. In contrast, there is more tolerance in the social structure of family groups in English (i.e. British and American) culture. Thus a son or a daughter after the age of eighteen is regarded as an independent adult, which is not the case in Arab culture.

(b) Pets: Many English families keep dogs or cats as pets; whereas dogs are considered in Arabic/Islamic culture as unclean animals like pigs.

(c) Taboos: In English culture, it is a social courtesy to greet a lady or a girl-friend with a kiss in public. This is taboo in Arab culture where kissing in public is allowed among Arab males only.

(d) Physical proximity and contact often reveal intimacy and degrees of formality. In British and American culture, however, facial expression is a more revealing indicator of interpersonal attitude.

(e) In Arab culture it is rather impolite to say 'no' to any request even if the feasibility of carrying it out is limited. Arabs usually answer in the affirmative by saying certain expressions like 'I will see, if God wills, I hope I can . . .', etc.), whereas English people would answer directly 'yes' or 'no', depending on the possibility or their intention of fulfilling the request.

(f) Manners of eating: Arabs drink only water or possibly soft drinks at table, whereas in English cultures it is common to drink alcohol.

(g) Selling and buying: Bargaining or asking the price of any commodity is an acceptable way of buying and selling in Arab culture, whereas it is rare in English culture.

Patterns of expression are also different in the two languages. These expressions are often used in conversational settings like hotel-lobbies, airport lounges, parties, coffee-shops, etc. The following are examples taken from English culture. The pupils can compare them with similar patterns found in Arab culture:

(a) Greetings, e.g.:   Hi, Good morning, etc.

(b) Introductions, e.g.:   May I introduce you to X?
                           Have you met X?
                           I want you to meet/know X.

(c) Interchanges, e.g.:   How do you do?
                           How are you? Fine, and you?
                           I'm glad to meet you,
                           It's nice to meet you, etc.

(d) Attention getting, e.g.	Excuse me/pardon me.
(e) Answering attention calls, e.g.	Yes sir, Yeah, Huh? What? What is it?
(f) Thanks, e.g.:	Thanks, Thank you, Many thanks
(g) Replying to thanks, e.g.:	You're welcome, Don't mention it, Not at all That's okay, etc.
(h) Requests for assistance, e.g.:	Would you mind . . .? Do you mind . . .? Could you . . .? I wonder if you'd mind . . . How about . . .? etc.
(i) Offers to help, e.g.:	How can I be of help to you? How can I assist you? What can I help you with? What can I do for you? May I help you? etc.
(j) Apologies, e.g.:	I'm sorry for being/having . . . Excuse me for being/having . . . Pardon me for being/having . . . I'm afraid that . . ., etc.
(k) Farewells, e.g.:	Good-bye/day/night, See you later/next . . . So long, Bye now, etc.

The understanding of cultural allusions will help pupils grasp the full meaning or function of the linguistic forms of the foreign language because they are often associated with the situation (i.e. social context) in which they occur. Pupils can clearly understand grammatical forms, but when they are used in conversational discourse they may interpret them differently unless they are aware of the cultural concepts underlying them. Culture and form, therefore complete and reinforce each other to make language meaningful. In short, with linguistic and cultural understanding, pupils can acquire communicative competence in English.

The understanding of cultural allusions will also help pupils to know how a society uses the language it speaks. This knowledge involves the concepts of acceptability and appropriateness which are essential for acquiring communicative competence in the foreign language, and it also helps pupils overcome problems resulting from cultural diversity. Pupils can compare features of the foreign culture with those of their native culture and, by doing so, they can comprehend cultural differences when they encounter them in learning the foreign language.

The pupils will also be able to adopt an appropriate style of speaking or writing the foreign language according to whether the communicative situation requires formal or other variations of language. By experiencing cultural conventions pupils can recognize more effectively the proper use of 'register' which, in turn affects linguistic content. For example, pupils will understand that a conversation between professionals would contain some words or expressions which are different from those used in a conversation between teenagers.

Because of its crucial role in foreign-language learning, awareness of the conventions of English and American culture needs to be taught hand in hand with language forms and functions. The teacher himself must be aware of the cultural behaviour so that he can interpret it for his pupils. Without this understanding, cultural explanation is impossible. This means that orientation training courses will be needed for language teachers.

7.2

Developing Cultural Knowledge

An understanding of the culture of the native speakers of the foreign language is therefore an essential requirement. To help pupils attain this goal, the syllabus as well as the language teacher should give due consideration to cultural items related to the community speaking the target language.

First, the foreign language syllabus must cater for the learning of culture and language (i.e. the social use of language). The teaching material should reflect, through its forms and patterns, the viewpoints and attitudes of the community concerned. In other words, the syllabus provides not only linguistic forms but also the notions, functions, experiences and situations that make them meaningful. The functional–notional syllabus is a good example of such material. It develops in the learner an ability to use the foreign language appropriately, and to understand its meanings and culture. With this particular syllabus, the pupils become familiar with the culture and they have an opportunity to observe the situations in which the language is used.

The process of developing cultural insights should be both systematic and incidental. The systematic mode involves control and gradation in learning cultural items. Thus at the early stage of learning, the teacher should explain only those cultural features that occur in learning the basic structures of the language. This is essential since pupils have not yet achieved an adequate command of the new language. But as they advance in the process of learning the language, cultural variations can be taught regularly through learning assignments and experiences. If motivation is to be sustained the syllabus should present easier areas of cultural content first so that pupils' interest in the target community evolves gradually and naturally. One of the main goals of developing cultural knowledge is to overcome false ideas and prejudice against the people who speak the target language. Instead correct cultural content should be learnt. This will foster positive attitudes in FL learners towards the people of the community so that they can appreciate their way of life. Such attitudes and empathy would make foreign language teaching and learning realize its major goal of developing understanding and co-operation among different nations.

The following strategies are appropriate for fostering awareness and interest in the foreign culture in the classroom:

(a) The environment of the classroom should reveal aspects of the target culture, this can be done through the use of bulletin boards, wall pictures, maps, magazines, newspapers, etc. For example, on bulletin boards pupils may display facts or information about the foreign country, highlight current events in that country, mount comic strips, newspaper clippings and topics of general interest, and copy out popular pieces of poetry, proverbs, anecdotes and the like. All these cultural items should be produced in the foreign language and be replaced with new ones at regular intervals.

(b) The teacher should provide the class with objects or pictures representative of the foreign country (e.g. money, costumes, stamps and pictures of historical or interesting places). These can be supplemented by appropriate books, stories and magazines so that pupils can familiarize themselves with the foreign culture.

(c) The language teacher may ask pupils as individuals or small groups to undertake projects such as drawing maps, writing timetables and dialogues. The teacher should select cultural activities that suit the pupils' learning level and interests. After completing the projects, the teacher conducts class discussion to arouse pupils' interest in the target culture. Such discussions should give pupils a chance to compare foreign cultural material with similar material in their native culture, or focus on the pupils' attitudes towards the people of the foreign culture and their way of life.

(d) The teacher can encourage his pupils to listen to songs and music of all types of the target culture, to have pen pals in the foreign country, to listen to recordings of lectures, or to watch illustrated talks on modern technology, etc. It is necessary to conduct such activities in English to enhance effective learning of both the culture and the language.

(e) Literature, in its broad sense, provides an effective instrument for developing cultural insights since it reflects the accomplishments of a community in various fields. It also illuminates its character, customs, registers. All these are varieties of culture.

(f) Experts in the target culture, or pupils who have recently visited an English-speaking country can be invited to talk about their experience in the foreign country. It is helpful to illustrate their talks with photographs, video films, etc. Such aids will arouse the learners' curiosity and interest and stimulate curiosity about the target culture.

Part Four

Teaching Language Skills

Introduction

The preceding Part dealt with the linguisitic and cultural elements of the English language; that is the sound, the vocabulary, the grammatical and the cultural systems. They are analysed separately for pedagogical purposes, and some techniques or learning activities are suggested for the teaching of each. However, these elements seldom exist autonomously outside the spoken or written forms of the language. They are utilized in the integrated communication skills which are traditionally categorized as listening, speaking, reading and writing. In fact, they are aspects of a unified system through which language operates. A knowledge of them is, therefore, necessary for interpreting or transmitting the language appropriately.

On the other hand, communicative abilities can be classified as receptive and productive skills. The former includes listening and reading, while the latter comprises speaking and writing. Although they will be treated separately, they are interdependent. Thus one may listen and speak or write, or read and write, and so on. This interrelationship is illustrated in the following diagram:

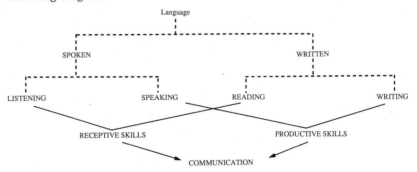

Adapted from Betty Wallace Robinett (1978) *Teaching English to Speakers of Other Languages*, McGraw-Hill, New York, p. 175.

One or more of these communicative skills are sometimes more emphasized than others. This depends on the objectives of the language course, the method of teaching and on the needs of the learners. For example, there are methods of teaching that stress speaking, reading, writing or aural comprehension or a combination of two or more of these skills. Whatever the objectives are, the FL teacher has to provide pupils with intensive activities to develop their communicative abilities. This requirement is essential in foreign language learning because the target language is taught in a foreign context. These activities, which simulate ordinary life outside the classroom situation will help the pupils to be fluent in their use of their skills. While these skills are integrative each of them will be examined separately for teaching purposes.

In discussing these skills, we shall follow the traditional sequence of listening, speaking, reading and writing. This ordering is significant since listening and speaking are two basic skills and are essential to acquiring communicative competence in the target language. In addition, learning these two skills first will reinforce the learning of the other two. The teacher has to pay attention to these skills from the beginning and should specify them as skills rather than knowledge. This necessitates systematic orientation in effective techniques of teaching so that he can deal with them appropriately.

Chapter Eight

Teaching Listening Comprehension

Introduction

Aural comprehension is the skill of listening, understanding and responding in an appropriate way. This skill provides the foundation for learning a foreign language. It is basic, for instance, for communicative methodology which emphasizes listening as a vital part of the language acquisition process. Thus unless the learner hears accurately and understands correctly, he will not be able to respond adequately. The skill of listening comprehension may also be regarded as the first step to achieving oral fluency and accuracy. In addition, the skill is needed in situations where oral response is not required. Instances include listening to a lecture, a discussion, a dialogue.

The teacher's task is to provide opportunities for the pupils to listen to living English used in everyday situations such as in shops, restaurants, public speeches and interviews. The teacher must also train the pupils to listen to and understand speech of native speakers of the target language. In this regard a lot of practice in listening is needed in order to increase the keenness of hearing so that pupils can (a) distinguish sounds, words and structures, (b) associate meanings with sounds, (c) infer meaning from speaker's discourse, (d) process messages, (e) understand conversational English in all kinds of speech situations and (f) understand, evaluate, organize, take notes and retrieve information.

Despite its importance as an essential language-learning skill, listening comprehension is probably the least stressed skill in the language classroom. The skill is often not taught or practised at all in English classes, especially in those where conventional methods and techniques are still used. This neglect causes frustration on the part of FL learners. Thus, after seven or eight years of English instruction, secondary school graduates find it difficult to understand spoken language or to follow a conversation with native speakers of the target language, though many of them have a good grasp of grammar, vocabulary, reading and composition. This may be attributed to a lack of listening materials; limited exposure to conversational English; shortcomings inherent in the audio-lingual method which considers this skill as a passive activity; and finally lack of well-trained teachers of English.

The following are the most important skills which the pupils will need for developing listening comprehension.

8.1

Requirements for Listening Practice

(a) The ability to distinguish English sounds such as /p/ and /b/, /e/ and /i/, /f/ and /v/, /θ/ and /ð/, /tʃ/ and /dʒ/, /s/ and /z/, /əʊ/ and /aʊ/, /ɜ:/ and /eə/, etc. Recognizing phonemic sounds is basic not only to the pupil's understanding of what he hears but also to this speaking.

(b) The ability to identify the intonational devices of English: rising intonation, falling intonation, stressed words versus unstressed words, the length of pauses, etc. For example a rising intonation may signal a question, word stress may direct the listener's attention to the most significant items in the utterance or text, whereas contractions are used for sentence rhythm.

One way of helping pupils become receptive to intonational devices is to expose them to the natural flow of English speech as in real conversations or talks.

(c) The ability to understand grammatical signals indicating:
1. Plural of nouns: books, churches,
2. Possessive of nouns: man's, men's
3. Third person singular (present tense) of verbs: sleeps, watches
4. Past tense of verbs: walked, lived, cleaned
5. Past participle of verbs: eaten, seen, driven
6. Present participle: reading, eating
7. Comparative of adjectives and adverbs: prettier, slower
8. Superlative of adjectives and adverbs: fastest, strongest
9. Derivational forms: act, active, activity; peace, pacify, peaceful
10. Concord or agreement: she sleeps, they sleep
11. Word order – lexical items: chocolate milk, milk chocolate, chair arm, armchair.
    functional items: they are, Are they? Where are they? I don't know where they are.
12. Question forms – Yes/no questions: Is your father a teacher? Could you play chess? Did you travel?
    Wh Questions: Who broke the window? Where does he live?
13. Negative forms – With the auxiliary do: He doesn't smoke. They didn't come to the party.
    Without the auxiliary do: They cannot speak French. I was not there. You must not talk in the classroom.
14. Sentence co-ordination with 'and', 'or', 'but', etc.
15. Sentence subordination with 'because', 'although', 'if', etc.

In addition, pupils must be aware of the grammatical arrangements including sentence structure (simple, compound, complex, negative and interrogative), order of noun modifiers, order of adverbial modifiers, modal auxiliaries, verb phrases, phrasal verbs, prepositions, articles, etc. Pupils should know, for example, that definite and indefinite articles change sound according to the word that follows them. Thus we say /ðə/ bus, /ði/ orange, an animal, an apple, a book, a university, etc.

(d) The ability to understand the meaning of the lexical items from the context or the situation being discussed (e.g., head of an organization, head of a table, etc.) In addition, pupils should be able to identify the key words in sentences, introductory words, attention claimers, formulas, idiomatic expressions, and hesitation words which occur in speech. Becoming familiar with such items would help pupils understand content and keep up with rapid speech.

(e) The ability to understand collocations of words. These words have some semantic relationships. Thus when a pupil hears a word like car, he expects to hear other words associated with it such as: driver, driving licence, insurance, garage, seat belt, petrol, etc. Similarly, when a pupil hears a definite or an indefinite article he expects a noun following it. When he hears the first part of a conditional sentence, he expects to hear in the second part one of the modal auxiliaries: will, may, can, might, could, should have, could have . . ., etc.

(f) The ability to understand cultural aspects implicit in the utterances. Recognizing these cultural concepts would increase pupils' understanding of the content.

(g) The ability to differentiate between written and spoken language. It is essential to recognize characteristics of spoken English such as reduction of vowel quality in words and the use of contractions for the sake of sentence melody. In addition to these general prerequisites, there are some specific factors which affect the process of developing listening skills. They can be categorized as follows:

1. The listening material. This should be:
    (i) of an appropriate level: preferably communicative, narrative or descriptive in order to develop concentration on specific detail, or the problem to be solved;
    (ii) carefully stated or designed;
    (iii) taught in a sequential manner, progressing from simple to more complex activities as pupils gain proficiency in the target language;
    (iv) suitable for pupils' age, sex, intelligence and interests;
    (v) compatible with the pupils' knowledge or social background;
    (vi) motivating to pupils' concentration and understanding;
    (vii) stimulating and not testing pupils' language abilities.

2. Acoustic environment. The listening setting should be away from distracting noise and interference, and provided with audio and visual aids, preferably a language laboratory where audio facilities are available.

3. The listener or pupil, who should be:
    (i) familiar with the target language in its various aspects: phonology, lexis, syntax and cohesion;
    (ii) aware of the theme or objective of the listening material or the topic under discussion;
    (iii) cognizant of the subject matter of the text;

(iv) able to recognize redundant clues such as false starts, attention claimers, connectors and function words;

(v) able to analyse and select, that is, to distinguish between main points, major ideas and supporting or minor ones;

(vi) used to radio listening or T.V. viewing;

(vii) familiar with reading/speaking habits;

(viii) trained in note-taking or summary making.

4. The speaker should have:

(i) good language ability;

(ii) clarity of pronunciation, accent, variation, voice, etc.;

(iii) comprehensible speed of delivery; the more normal, the easier to understand spoken discourse;

(iv) to some extent, prestige and personality.

The complicated nature of the listening comprehension process requires, in addition to the elements listed above, regular listening practice, adequate exposure to authentic language, and a favourable attitude towards the language and its speakers. Moreover, listening comprehension as a skill should be taken into account in examinations so as to heighten the pupils' interest in the activity. Without this interest, listening comprehension will continue to receive little attention.

8.2

Levels of Listening Comprehension

Training pupils in listening comprehension involves three levels of activity: elementary, intermediate and advanced. At the elementary level, pupils learn to identify sound patterns, meanings of words, phrases or expressions and to recognize grammatical elements or communicative acts. At the intermediate level they practise aural comprehension to select from short conversations the elements which give the gist of a message. At the advanced level, aural material is used to deduce meanings or outlines from a lengthy spoken discourse. The following model activities may stimulate teachers to produce their own. They are sequenced to meet different levels of learning or language proficiency.

(a) Listening for stress, rhythm and intonation. Lively dialogues and the normal conversations of native speakers of English are useful to familiarize pupils with the sounds or features of pauses, stress, rhythm, intonation and emotional overtones (e.g. anger). These are important because of their effect on the spoken language as opposed to the written form which the pupils may already recognize.

Foreign-language learners frequently fail to comprehend oral utterances because of the tendency to reduce and run together all unstressed syllables. To remedy this situation, practice with vowel reduction, minimal pairs and word stress is needed from the beginning, so that pupils can identify and discriminate between sounds.

(b) Games and competitions are another kind of listening exercise which help pupils recognize the sounds of words, word classes, word meaning, idioms, colloquialisms, false starts, attention claimers, etc. Activities that require quick word recognition are useful in sharpening listening skill, therefore pupils should have frequent exercises in the phonological, syntactic and semantic codes of English.

(c) Closely related to word recognition is identification of key words. In this activity, pupils listen to a single sentence, then they are asked to give orally, or to write, the key words – subject, verb, object, and other elements. For example, 'The teachers went to the conference to learn some teaching techniques.' Key words to be identified would be: teachers, conference, learn, techniques. This simple activity develops the listening skill because it encourages pupils to focus on key words so as to grasp the basic message, and to disregard less important information.

(d) Another listening comprehension activity is dictation. This technique is an excellent exercise to call pupils' attention to the occurrence of words in sentences, and expand their knowledge of vocabulary. The procedure of giving a dictation goes like this: pupils listen, first to the passage read (by the teacher or on tape) at normal speed, then the passage is read with pauses for pupils to write. When it is completed, pupils are instructed to check their dictation as they listen to the passage for the third time.

A variation of this technique is question/answer practice. In this exercise a list of questions is dictated, either by the teacher or on tape, then pupils answer them in writing.

Another technique to help pupils record what they hear for retention is multiple-choice exercises where they are given a sentence orally, and then required to match one of its words from options provided. For example: 'I have never seen such an array of beautiful flowers'. Which word best matches *array*: bouquet? exhibition? variety? etc. The problem with such exercises lies in the difficulty of designing them. They need adequate material, careful preparation and a competent teacher who can handle them efficiently.

(e) Listening for drawing. This activity requires vocabulary related to shape and orientation and some preparation. The procedure is simple. The teacher or the speaker tells the class to draw figures and objects in certain specified places and ways in order to produce a particular picture. No gesturing is allowed. When the task is finished, pupils can compare their drawing with the original. If competition is desired, the pupils whose drawings are closest to the original can be granted marks.

(f) Listening to short interviews. This activity can be done in class with pupils grouped in pairs, in the following sequence:

(i) The teacher reads to the pupils a passage, about five minutes in length, involving a particular topic such as a field trip, recreation in spare time or in vacations, and so on.

(ii) The teacher asks the class questions in written form, in order to help pupils focus their attention on the content of the listening material.

(iii) After that the teacher reads the passage again so that pupils can get most of the answers. But he must make it clear to them that they are not just to answer the questions, but to use them for interview purposes.

(iv) To make the activity more rewarding as well as enjoyable the teacher may have the pupils use their ingenuity to suggest other questions or to interview native speakers of English in the neighbourhood, or at informal gatherings.

(g) Listening to dialogues. Another useful technique is the use of short taped conversations or dialogues between native speakers of English talking in everyday situations (such as asking for a room in a hotel, ordering a meal in a restaurant, shopping, etc.) where language, with its pauses and fillers, idioms, and so forth, is reflected. For this activity, the following procedure is recommended:

  (i) The pupils listen to the recording, answer general comprehension questions and discuss new vocabulary.

  (ii) The pupils listen to the recording for the second time, and write down interesting and useful expressions.

  (iii) The teacher discusses with them functions and expressions, and corrects mistakes.

  (iv) Finally, pupils working in pairs may try to write a dialogue similar to the one they heard on the tape.

As a variation of this activity, pupils can practise taking or leaving messages, making appointments and getting information via the telephone.

This exercise can be conducted as follows:

  (i) The teacher groups the class in pairs and instructs them to sit back-to-back in order to 'phone' each other.

  (ii) Pupils are to write down the information they receive so that they can repeat the message accurately.

  (iii) While practising the activity, the teacher walks round monitoring the pupils' conversations.

  (iv) Depending on the level of the class, the teacher may assign the tasks the pupils are to practise. Thus he may suggest to them dialling a doctor for an appointment, an airline for a flight arrival, a tour agency for booking and the like.

(h) The teacher can also ask the pupils to make phone calls to native speakers of English in agencies or companies. They can inquire about any information that interests them.

(i) Radio, videotapes and films: Using radio programmes and videotapes as sources of learning is somewhat difficult because FL learners may not have a clear idea of the cultural information needed to understand a particular situation. This technique also requires careful preparation and specific guidance. The teacher must study thoroughly the taped broadcast material, and check the validity of the films he intends to present in classes. Nevertheless, these sources are excellent listening materials using live language and a variety of topics, situations and speakers. Films should be short (fifteen minutes or so in length), without subtitles, interesting and providing a natural context to help pupils listen attentively. Films should also be sequenced from easier to more difficult, so that pupils will be continually challenged but not frustrated.

Before showing the film, the teacher supplies the class, with background to the film and some explanations depending on the complexity of the topic. Subsequently, the teacher gives the pupils some questions to answer about the incidents and events of the film. After that, the teacher shows the class the film for the second time. If time allows, he may conduct a class discussion by using the material of the film as the topic of the discussion. This is to make sure that the information has been heard and understood correctly by the pupils.

The radio and T.V. programmes should also be short and of general interest such as lectures, talk shows, weather reports, cookery programmes, and the like. The teacher, however, should check the validity of the taped segment before presenting it in class. Appropriate questions about the content of that particular tape should be given to pupils in advance. The teacher is also to prime the class on who is speaking to whom, the nature of their relationship, and their expectations in the situation, etc.

Alternatively, if the necessary equipment is not available in class, the teacher can assign pupils to listen to the broadcasts of radio stations, or to watch a television documentary and take notes or record opinions to be discussed later in class.

(j) Listening for gist. In this exercise pupils listen to a whole passage with the aim of extracting the main idea from it. They are not expected to concentrate on specific words, or phrases or secondary information.

The procedure for this activity is simple. The teacher plays the tape once only. Pupils then tell him in a few short sentences what the passage is about. The objective is to help them become good listeners. Pupils can make notes as they listen so that they can retell, in their own words, what they have understood and can remember. If the listening passage contains a problem that can be solved by pupils, the teacher may conduct a class discussion using the notes taken while listening to the material. This technique encourages them to talk and argue about what they have heard.

There are many other activities which lend themselves to listening practice. Here are some of them:
1. Telling a story and asking pupils some questions about it.
2. Reading a poem, a passage or a playlet and asking pupils to state specific points.
3. Simulating telephone conversations.
4. Conducting mock interviews, and writing ideas and facts.
5. Attending lectures or seminars and reporting to the class the main points or ideas.
6. Problem-solving about topics of general interest.
7. Listening to news bulletins on the radio or watching television programmes and recounting headlines.
   The teacher should consult language teaching books for other listening drills and exercises.

8.3

General Procedures and Techniques

The preceding sections presented various ways of teaching listening comprehension which depend on the type and aim of each aural exercise. There are, however, other steps that should be taken into consideration in the teaching process. These procedures are necessary to the presentation of any listening activity. They are as follows:

1. The listening material should not include structures and vocabulary beyond the pupils' level of proficiency.

2. Before presenting the listening material, the teacher must tell the class the purpose of the activity, the nature of the task they are going to undertake. He should give a brief introduction to give them a chance to anticipate what they are about to hear.

3. The number of times the pupils need to hear the passage depends on the length and difficulty of the passage, the nature and purpose of the set task, and the level of pupils' proficiency.

4. Pupils may work on the required task as they listen to the selection.

5. When the pupils have completed the required task, the teacher may either read the answers to them or provide an answer key and have them correct their own answers.

6. The teacher must check the pupils' progress in order to help them deal with the difficulty of the listening material or the questions to be answered, etc.

It may be noted that many other listening materials can be prepared for pupil practice in this area. However, it is hoped that the guidelines presented in this chapter may be useful to the EFL teacher in working out a syllabus for a listening comprehension class. But it has to be stressed that listening comprehension should always be viewed as a developing ability, so the listening activities are to be sequenced and graded.

8.4
Testing Listening Comprehension

Although communicative methodology emphasizes aural–oral skills, often English syllabuses do not focus on a sequential and methodical development of the listening skill, and do not define levels of competence. The skill is treated marginally in the teaching–learning processes whether the syllabus is structural or notional–functional. In such a situation, listening evaluation tends to be ignored. Thus the listening element is excluded from all types of school examinations. Only written examinations are given. Aural-oral fluency tests are combined in a classroom mark which takes into account attendance, homework, classroom participation. Teachers do not attempt to assess the pupils' ability in listening and speaking skills at the end of each learning stage. The skill receives little attention either in practice or testing.

Nevertheless, foreign language teachers must experiment with different methods of evaluating listening comprehension. They can follow several testing techniques to assess pupils' general proficiency in English. Here are some suggested techniques which test different abilities ranging from recognising sound patterns to comprehending factual content or making inferences.

(a) Understanding individual words.
   This test is meant for the elementary or intermediate stage. It is designed to assess the understanding of individual words in isolation or in the context of sentences. The teacher says a word and points to a picture or figure. Pupils give a 'True' or 'False' response accordingly. It is

important that teachers do not repeat the word in order to retain the attention of pupils.

(b) Recognizing sentences.

There are several ways in which pupils can demonstrate their ability to understand the meaning of sentences or utterances. Some of these techniques are the following:

1. Carrying out an action
2. Executing a series of rapid commands
3. Drawing pictures on the chalkboard or on sheets of paper
4. Acting in response to a series of directions
5. Using objects on the magnetic or the flannel board
6. Playing games or charades
7. Using visual cues
8. Giving equivalents in the mother tongue, etc.

(c) Testing structure signals.

In this technique pupils listen to a series of sentences, live or taped, containing certain structure signals, e.g.: subject/object, singular/plural, pronouns–personal, etc. As pupils hear the sentences, they write the required item.

(d) Understanding short oral passages.

In this test pupils listen to a variety of short oral passages, live or recorded, such as short plays and conversations. They are expected to infer certain information from what they have just heard, or to answer true–false statements or multiple-choice questions. The teacher may also give the pupils direct questions to be answered in writing. These are useful to evaluate the general comprehension of pupils. The questions should be distributed before the listening passage is played.

(e) Testing the understanding of extended passages.

This test is applicable to advanced stages of learning. The pupils listen to extended passages: recordings of speeches, radio plays, discussions on important issues, and the like. The task assigned to the students is to take notes, or to write a brief outline of the main points.

Chapter Nine

Teaching
Speaking

Introduction

Learning to speak is a lengthy, complex process. Many foreign language teachers realize that fluency in speaking is the most difficult skill to develop. In addition to linguistic and cultural knowledge, there are other requirements that should be available in order to develop this skill. They include the following:

(a) A competent teacher who is fluent in conversation.
(b) Appropriate classroom atmosphere, which is conducive to oral communicative acts, and where pupils feel at ease and relaxed.
(c) Ample opportunity for pupil participation.
(d) Clear objectives in speaking so that pupils can think of the ideas they wish to express.
(e) A knowledge of the appropriate functional expressions.
(f) A variety of learning activities including manipulative drills, guided conversation, communicative practice and free oral work such as discussion groups, debates, panel discussions, skills competitions, etc.
(g) Sensitivity to any change in the situation in which communicative operations are taking place.
(h) Contextualized language in terms of who is speaking to whom, where and why.

All of these requirements are essential for the development of the speaking skill. Probably for this reason this skill is frequently neglected or often conducted poorly in English classes. As a compensation for this shortcoming, emphasis is usually placed on drilling patterns, reading passages and answering comprehension questions. All these activities are controlled by the teacher and have no natural context of their own. In such situations, pupils speak very little English, and when they speak, much of what they say will be in answer to questions from the teacher.

Learning to speak English is more effectively achieved by speaking than by listening or reading. Pupils, therefore, must have the opportunity to express their likes and dislikes, to talk about their interests, etc., in living natural English. Without this training in the productive skill of speech, pupils' ability to communicate in spoken English will be meagre despite all knowledge of rules of pronunciation, of grammar and of sentence formation.

To help pupils to develop speaking ability, this chapter will describe procedures of teaching speech as a communicative activity. At the same time, it will suggest some activities that encourage pupils to exchange ideas spontaneously, and to practise fluency in questions while focusing attention on the information instead of the linguistic forms carrying that information.

Three components may be distinguished in teaching oral communication: mechanical oral practice, meaningful oral work, and free oral production.

9.1

Stage I: Mechanical Practice

The first step in teaching speaking is to train pupils in sound discrimination, oral vocabulary, verb forms and grammatical patterns. These elements are necessary to acquire a basic knowledge of linguistic competence. Thus pronuncation should be stressed from the beginning because habits acquired at the start of language study are often difficult to change later on. Pupils, therefore, must practise hearing and understanding what is said or heard and must pronounce it correctly.

This activity is best carried out in the language laboratory where pupils can work at their own pace. They record some sentences, after a model, and then listen to each recording in order to correct any pronunciation problems. They continue this process until they gain some insight into the nature of the phonological rules of English.

At the same time, the teacher should draw pupils' attention to the rules of grammar and of sentence formation. These elements are interdependent and should be developed concurrently. Pupils must, for instance, know that a word may have different pronunciations or meanings in different situations. In addition, they must know the rules of question formation and other types of sentences (statements, imperative, negative, passives, etc.). This is meant to help pupils differentiate grammatical from ungrammatical utterances, so that they can speak English fluently as they progress in language learning. However, the vocabulary, structures and other language patterns should be carefully selected and of high frequency. The speaking activities should be controlled in order to eliminate the possibility of errors in pupils' responses.

Examples of Mechanical Drills

There are many types of manipulative drill where there is complete control of the pupils' responses. Typical examples of these are repetition, 'mim-mem' and substitution drills. Here are some examples:

Teacher	:	My book was lost.
Class	:	My book was lost.
Teacher	:	(giving a cue for substitution), The English
Class	:	The English book was lost, etc.
Teacher	:	The girls are playing.
Pupil	:	What are the girls doing? etc.

Teacher	:	Waleed is going to America on his vacation. He's wealthy.
Pupil	:	Waleed is wealthy enough to go to America on his vacation. (Followed by choral repetition, etc.)

Teacher	:	English _____ easy.
Pupil	:	I thought English would be easy, but it turned out to be difficult.

Teacher	:	Ali is playing.
Pupil	:	What is Ali doing?

The foregoing drills are simple types of manipulative skills. There are many other pattern practice drills. These exercises are structurally controlled so that the pupils always know beforehand the pattern they are required to illustrate. Their main function is to help pupils acquire the skill of producing the sounds and structures of the language automatically. But the overuse of mechanical drills may induce boredom and a distaste for language learning. The teacher, therefore, should be careful in handling such drills.

9.2

Stage 2: Meaningful Oral Work

At the second stage of learning to speak English, the structural controls are progressively relaxed. Having automatic control over basic patterns by means of the habituation process, and having increased their linguistic competence through practice in various types of manipulative drills, pupils can handle meaningful activities fairly well. The pupils now understand what they are saying structurally and semantically. But there is no real communication taking place because there is still control of the response and the speakers do not add new information as they are still subject to some restraints. Furthermore, the initiative is still left with the teacher or with the group leader.

This stage introduces the pupils to social formulas: greetings, introductions, complaints, asking for information, etc. It also gives them expressions with which to express their ideas creatively. It produces few incorrect sentences, and these are corrected by members of the group, not by the teacher.

Procedures and examples

For drilling guided oral fluency, the teacher provides the class with the situation and content of what is to be said, and pupils communicate within this general framework. Topics and exercises should follow closely the interests of the pupils in order to encourage pupil–pupil interaction and to make English classes a lively and cheerful experience. Material can be drawn from different sources such as textbooks, pupils' compositions, English newspapers or magazines, language games, classroom objects, and the like. It is also important to make situations as concrete as possible. Persons, places and things should be named rather than referred to as generic concepts. Contextualization highlights the social setting of language use. It also motivates the pupils because they are practising the language as it is actually used by native speakers.

The teacher should make the following points clear:

Setting: Where are the people talking? What sounds do they hear? What is the weather like? and so on. This will help pupils visualize the scene and stimulate them to talk.

Action: What actions initiate or terminate the conversation, and what do the participants do during the activity? Are they standing, sitting, walking or so? How are they reacting. This will inject humour and liveliness into the classroom situation.

Emotion: Pupils must be encouraged to express their feelings and opinions. The pupils will feel the vitality and expressiveness of English.

Function: Pupils should know why someone says something and what it means. Understanding the purpose makes the drill meaningful and eliminates habituation practice.

With these points in mind, the teacher has to explain structural items that the pupils may use in the questions and answers. And, if the teacher wants to introduce new patterns, it is best to drill them thoroughly before using them in the activity.

Once the teacher has explained procedural steps and the teaching method, including the rearrangement of the class to meet the requirements of the activity and to encourage everyone to participate, he starts drilling the speaking activity. The methods suggested for this stage are guessing games, simple role-playing and dialogues, and the like: Here are some examples:

Example 1:

Teacher	:	Some pupils are playing
Pupil 1	:	Who is playing?
Pupil 2	:	Ali and Sami are playing.

Example 2: Question and answer exchanges between the pupils

Pupil 1	:	What time did you come to school?
Pupil 2	:	I came at eight
Pupil 3	:	Shall we go swimming?
Pupil 4	:	No, let's go shopping.

Example 3: Dialogue adaptation

Pupil 1	:	Why didn't you come on time?
Pupil 2	:	Well, I couldn't find the way at first
Pupil 1	:	Did you ask somebody?
Pupil 2	:	Yes, a policeman.

Example 4: Short conversations

Pupil 1	:	Did you go to Egypt last summer?
Pupil 2	:	Yes, I visited the pyramids and Alexandria.
Pupil 1	:	How was your trip?
Pupil 2	:	Fantastic. Egypt is a beautiful and exciting country.

The pupils select different places and vary the adjectives accordingly.

Example 5: Directed discourse in which the teacher guides the pupils

Teacher	:	Ali, ask Sameer where he went last night.
Ali	:	Where did you go?
Sameer	:	To the cinema.
Teacher	:	What film did you see?
Sameer	:	Jaws.
Teacher	:	Ahmad, ask Sameer if it was frightening.

Ahmad	:	Was it frightening?
Sameer	:	Yes.
Teacher	:	Tell us three things about Jaws.
Sameer	:	O.K. . . .

In the above example, the teacher is setting up a situation that makes the pupils do the work. The teacher is not asking the questions; he is guiding or directing pupil A to ask pupil B. His main concern is to encourage pupils to use their imagination and to talk about their own experience or opinions.

Example 6: Oral guessing games. Such games provide pupils with good practice in formulating questions, a skill that does not receive sufficient attention in English classes. Questions are usually put by the teacher or written in the textbook. Here is an example: What is it?

In this activity, a pupil is asked to leave the classroom. The class then selects a small object, such as a piece of chalk, and hides it. The pupil returns and tries to discover its location by asking the class yes/no questions, using the following prepositions: in front of, near, far from, on . . . left, in, on, under, between, etc.

The pupil moves around, asking questions from different positions in the room until he discovers the location of the object.

Example 7: Prepared talks. The teacher assigns a topic or a choice of topics for a prepared talk. The pupils write an outline of what they want to say. This is to encourage thoughtful preparation. Then they give their talks in the class without using the notes they have written.

As a variation of this technique pupils may talk about what they did in the summer, last night, etc.

Example 8: Playlets. The teacher divides the class into appropriate groups. Each group is asked to prepare a sketch using their ideas and making use of the teacher's suggestions. When the sketches are ready, individual groups present them to other members of the class, or to other classes or to the English language club.

Example 9: Informative sentences. The teacher writes on the chalkboard a sentence or two that can evoke a variety of questions from the pupils, e.g. 'Yesterday I was swimming when a boy shouted for help . . .' This sentence may prompt questions like:

What was the time?
Who was swimming with you?
Where were you swimming?
How was the sea?
Was the boy small or big?
How far was he swimming?
Was anybody else with him?
How did you rescue him?
Where did you take him to?

Example 10: Rank order. The teacher (with class participation) writes on the blackboard some activities which one might do at a weekend or on Thursday evening, etc. Examples: watch television, go to the cinema, go swimming, visit friends, etc. The teacher then asks pupils to indicate their order of preference. The activity may go like this:

Teacher	:	Ali, which activity do you like best?
Ali	:	Swimming
Teacher	:	Why?
Ali	:	I like sports.

The teacher then continues with the other options in the same manner. As a variation of this activity, there are categories of preference. In this activity, the teacher writes the categories of TV programmes on the blackboard and asks the pupils to state their favourite category and why they prefer it.

9.3
Stage 3: Free Oral Production

By the third stage of learning to speak, the pupils have the basic machinery to say whatever they want or feel and to tell others what they did. However, the teacher has to set up the situation or to provide the stimuli that arouse the pupils' interest. Visual aids and props are good tools to set up class discussions, dialogues and other speaking activities. Moreover, the teacher has to fit the oral activities to the pupils' own cultural background in order to meet their interests and to motivate them to participate in the activity. The teacher also has to prepare the material adequately as free discussions are likely to fail if he hasn't planned them carefully in advance. In fact the success of free conversation depends on four elements: careful preparation by the teacher and the pupils; the silence of the teacher during the activity; the availability of interesting topics that stimulate pupils to participate; and confidence in their ability to communicate.

9.4
Procedures and Techniques

Training at this stage is best done with group work in problem-solving and role-playing activities, conversation classes, dramatization and the like. In such activities group work is favoured as it is more motivating and more useful for oral fluency. It also meets the problem of large classes with over thirty pupils. The teacher can divide the class into appropriate groups appointing a group leader for each. He then assigns the activity or task. An appropriate time is allowed to the groups to discuss the problem, after which the pupils meet together as a large group to summarize their conclusions.

However, if the class is too large, the pupils may place their desks in a semi-circle, with the rostrum as the head desk. This arrangement involves the pupils in a series of activities and encourages everyone to participate. Another possible class organization is to pair the pupils off to interview each other about a particular topic. It is left to the discretion of the teacher to decide which class arrangements suits the situation and meets the requirements of the activity.

With these organizational considerations in mind, the teacher proceeds to conduct the activity. The teacher supplies first the general topic for assignment, leaving the class with responsibility for generating the details and supporting material. If the teacher feels that the class has not been sufficiently motivated by the oral presentation, he can provide the necessary stimuli for promoting the activity. For example, he may give the class notes containing most of the vocabulary and structures useful to the activity or he may assign the topic for the next session so that the pupils have time to think about it, as it is often difficult for them to talk in English at a moment's notice. The teacher has to instruct the class that no one will be allowed to take a dominant part in the activity, and everyone will be given the opportunity to speak.

The teacher then asks the pupils to avoid those questions that are normally answered by Yes/No as they do not further the activity. Instead, pupils should use open-ended questions (e.g. how, why and what) that require the answering pupils to give an opinion, information, a reason or an emotional reaction, etc. Pupils should be encouraged to assist each other so that the activity never degenerates into questions and answers between them.

The teacher should not frequently interrupt the flow of the speaking activity in order to correct mistakes. Immediate correction destroys self-confidence and consequently inhibits pupils' desire to speak. The teacher may tactfully mediate to clear up a problem that the pupils have failed to explain adequately, but his participation should be limited and restricted only to errors that lead to miscomprehension. The main concerns are developing pupils' motivation to speak and increasing fluency and ease of expression. What is said is not particularly important. Speaking English is the primary concern. The teacher can help his pupils achieve this objective through a series of communicative interaction activities. Here are some examples:

Dialogues

Dialogues are beneficial in the development of the speaking skill. They provide an effective starting point for training in free and creative communication. There are different types of dialogue and each of them can serve as the basis of spontaneous interaction.

The teacher has to initiate the topic of the dialogue. This is essential for sound classroom learning, and to avoid confusion. Props and teaching aids such as diagrams, grocery lists and the like can serve the classes for conversation.

As an example of establishing a situation for building up a dialogue, the teacher may give the class a short account such as: 'It is nine o'clock in the morning. Sameer, Muneer and Nabeel are talking about going swimming. Sameer wants to do an errand first, and so does Muneer. So they agree to go swimming at eleven o'clock.'

The dialogue may go like this:

Nabeel	:	Hey boys,
Sameer	:	Yes.
Nabeel	:	I was looking for you.
Muneer	:	What for?
Nabeel	:	About going swimming.
Muneer	:	A good idea. It's hot today.
Sameer	:	But I'm going down town, I want to buy a book.
Muneer	:	So am I. I want to get some sugar and rice from the supermarket.
Nabeel	:	Then we can meet at eleven.
Sameer:	:	That's fine. We have plenty of time.
Muneer	:	Yes
Nabeel	:	O.K. goodbye.

Muneer : Bye
Sameer : Bye-bye.

To make the exercise successful, the teacher has to prepare the situations carefully before the class begins.

Interviews

There are different types of interview assignments. One technique is to bring a pupil to the front of the class to be interviewed by the class, about his feelings, family, opinions on a particular issue, etc. The pupil must give frank answers, but may pass on any question he does not wish to answer. The questions should be based on known vocabulary and structures. In answering questions, the pupil should give short answers and then add extra information to show that he has understood or not understood, and to keep the interview going. Interviewer pupils should be encouraged to base their questions on the extra information the pupil gives. Example:

Interviewer : How long have you been in your present job?
Applicant : About three years. I started working there just after I graduated.
Interviewer : Do you use English much in your work?
Applicant : Not much at all, because we don't deal with English speakers, and all our data is in Arabic.

Interview exercises can be graded in order of difficulty. The easiest type is to give pupils a list of questions and for them to prepare their answers at home. Another is to give pupils headings and cue words and ask them to frame their own questions. Examples:

An interview for a job
  Personal Information:
  (a) country of origin, (b) age, (c) marital status, (d) children's ages, (e) parents, (f) health, (g) hobbies and interests, (h) sports.

  Qualifications:
  (a) education, where? degree? (b) training courses, (c) foreign languages, (d) experience, number of years, (e) type of work, (f) why leave previous job?, (g) special qualifications?

  This job:
  (a) reasons for wanting the job, (b) expected salary, (c) willing to do overtime? (d) working conditions, etc.

After interviewing some pupils, the class confers to decide which applicant is best qualified for the job.

The activity can be played as a press conference with the pupils acting as newspaper reporters and the teacher as a famous person, a history-book writer, and the like. The teacher may also ask the pupils to interview people outside class and to report the findings of their interviews to the class. Such techniques are effective in providing practice in spoken communication.

Role-playing

Role-playing is a variation of interviews in which the pupils are presented with a situation which involves conflict. They attempt to make the problem clear by playing the roles of the participants in the situation. The situation can be realistic, humorous, and imaginative. The following procedures can be followed in conducting this activity.

1. The teacher explains the situation and describes the action to be accomplished.

2. The teacher gives general information they don't have. This information is necessary for the role play.

3. Cultural expressions, technical vocabulary or certain structural patterns may be given if the teacher feels that they are needed to develop the activity. For example, a participant must know how to express anger, apologies and the like in living English.

4. The teacher assigns the roles which should all have fictitious names. It is more effective if the roles are fitted to the personality of the players.

5. If the activity contains a few roles, the teacher may ask several groups in the class to perform it simultaneously as group work. The following situations are samples of role playing activity.

   (a) You would like to borrow some money from a bank. The bank manager is reluctant to lend you the money. Try to persuade him to give you the loan.
   (b) Your son gets into trouble in school all the time. You are called to see the headmaster who is displeased with his behaviour. Try to convince him that your child is an angel at home.
   (c) Give excuses to the teacher for not having completed a long-term assignment. Try to get an extension. The teacher is opposed to it, as you have been known to do this before.
   (d) You want to watch a particular channel on television and the rest of the family wants to watch something else. Try to get your way – constructively, giving logical reasons. Other members of the group should give counter-arguments.

There are many other role-playing exercises which allow pupils to express their emotions and to interact in lifelike situations and help in improving oral proficiency.

Problem-solving

This is an effective technique of communicative interaction activities. It is particularly useful for speaking in free discussion as it involves group work.

The teacher first divides the class into two or three major groups. Within each group he forms appropriate subgroups of mixed ability consisting of four or five members, depending on the size of the class. After that the teacher presents them with a problem and some alternative solutions from which they have to choose one. The closer the problem to the pupils' interests and prior experience, the more successful the exercise will be. Discussion takes place initially between the small groups, and later with larger groups. Finally a full-class debate follows in the classroom. The following will illustrate this technique.

The problem: 'The people of a medium-sized town want to build a new school.

But they argue whether to build it inside or outside the town.'

The class is assumed to be divided into two major groups, A and B.

The groups in Category A will discuss the advantages of building the school inside the town in the light of the following points: shorter distances and less time to get to school, money wasted on pupils' travel, plenty of public transport, close to library, hospital, housing facilities, etc.

The groups in category B are against town centre location. They argue from these points of view: noise and air pollution, traffic dangers, less housing available for teachers, no room for future expansion, no room for sports field, etc. . . .

After posing the problem, the individual groups discuss it. The teacher should not intervene unless someone gets stuck or if pupils do not understand a point. Discussion and exchange of information is the object of the activity. Finally the whole class arrives at a solution of the problem posed.

Debates

Class debates are effective in developing speaking skills especially if the topics are of interest to the pupils. Examples include debates about aspects of their cultural and political life, or about current events or subjects of general interest. Some topics:

- Married women should not work for companies or in offices.
- Youngsters should not be allowed to drive cars.
- Monthly tests in secondary schools should be abolished.

The topic chosen must be clearly stated and controversial so that pupils can take a stand for or against it.

After selecting the subject, the teacher divides the class into two teams with different abilities. Each team then elects a captain or leader to co-ordinate the work among the members of his team. The teacher assigns the subject some time before the debate takes place. He may give the pupils key words and expressions which can be used in the debate. The pupils prepare at home some notes and ideas about what they might say.

When running the debate, the teacher will let the group supporting the motion begin the discussion. They present their position in detail. After that, the other team replies. The teacher observes whether the members of the two teams are given the chance to participate. He also makes notes for later comments when the debate is over.

Other interaction activities include discussion sessions, conversation classes and classroom drama. All these oral activities help pupils develop their communicative abilities. The teacher, however, has to select only those that are within the range of his pupils' ability and interest. This will motivate pupils and make them feel the vitality and expressiveness of the language they are learning.

Chapter 10

Teaching Reading

Introduction

Reading can be described as the process of extracting meaning from printed or written material. That is, the ability to decode meaning from graphic symbols as illustrated by Goodman (1967, p. 113): (1) graphic code → decoding → meaning. Reading according to this thesis is similar to listening where the listener tries to decipher the spoken symbols to comprehend the speech.

Reading, however, involves a whole series of subsidiary skills. These include the recognition of the alphabetic system, the correlation of the graphic symbols with formal linguistic elements, as well as intellectual comprehension and mechanical eye movement. Each of these elements may present a problem to the foreign language learner. Thus he may encounter difficulties with sound symbol relationships. In English there is not a one-to-one correlation between the sound and the written symbol. Examples are:

– the sound of 'c' in words like car, core or city;
– the different sounds of the grapheme (gh) in enough, through, night and hiccough;
– the final silent (e) which signals a change in vowel sound as in mad/made, not/note, bit/bite, cut/cute, etc.

There is also the problem of reading direction. Arabic is read from right to left, the opposite direction to English. Cultural aspects are another problem which requires guidance on the part of the teacher when training the pupils in the reading skill.

However, pupils should not start any kind of reading before they are familiar with the material they are about to read. A child is not expected to read words he has not heard and said several times. He must not be overwhelmed at the beginning. Instead, he must be given graded materials beginning with pictures to identify the reading of simple sentences, paragraphs, and short passages. Furthermore, the content and vocabulary should be of some relevance to the pupils' environment and interest. As the pupils progress in learning the language, the level of the reading texts also develops.

There is also the question of teaching the mechanics of reading such as the alphabet, the direction of reading, pauses, reading speed and English sounds. Attention to all these mechanical aspects is necessary to develop reading skills properly.

10.1
The Importance of Reading

The main goal of teaching reading is to train pupils to read efficiently and quickly enough to get information or meaning from written material rapidly and with full understanding. Besides this general aim, there are other reasons for reading such as the following:

(a) At the initial stages of learning the foreign language, reading serves primarily to introduce basic linguistic forms – phonemes, words, structures, sentence patterns and language functions – in an appropriate context. It also helps pupils to recognize visual symbols, appreciate sentence rhythm, acquaint themselves with English spelling and improve their pronunciation. Reading, at this elementary stage, takes the form of oral practice or rote recitation. Pupils usually read aloud words, sentences, short paragraphs, simple dialogues, songs and the like.

(b) After grasping the essentials of sound–symbol relationships and having mastered the basic techniques of reading, pupils are guided to read and comprehend longer selections. The objective is to develop their ability in comprehending specific information implied in the reading text, and to broaden their knowledge of more vocabulary, new ideas, cultural content, language functions and expressions, etc., and to reinforce the basic knowledge they have acquired in the foreign language. Furthermore, reading serves to integrate a variety of language activities, namely listening, speaking and writing. Thus pupils' reading experience provides topics for oral discussion and writing. Similarly, listening to stories, poems or reports will enable pupils to develop their ability in aural comprehension.

(c) Individualized reading gives pupils the freedom to select what they wish to read. Here, reading skills have practical or recreational purposes. Pupils may sometimes read books, magazines and journals either for enjoyment or to acquire general information, and widen their background knowledge. Consequently they must be motivated to continue reading in and outside school.

(d) Reading helps foreign language learners improve their English competence partly because it involves linguistic aspects and cultural allusions, and partly because it provides them with real-life situations. They have familiarity with such items as the street, the market, the club, the seashore, the office, the hospital, where the language is often used.

(e) Reading forms a tool of communication in addition to listening and speaking. People who have no opportunity to talk with native speakers of the target language can have an access through reading to their literature, and consequently understand more about their civilization. In this sense, reading is the window through which they can see other cultures and gain more general or specific knowledge.

(f) In the Arab world, the reading skill is often more important than any language skills. This is because English is taught more for business or academic purposes than for daily communication.

10.2

Types of Reading

Reading falls into two major categories: intensive and extensive. The former is a classroom activity carried on under the guidance of the teacher. It is mainly concerned with texts and involves focusing upon new words, structures, expressions, functions, pronunciation and cultural insights. It is carefully guided so that thorough understanding of the content may be achieved.

However, reading which constitutes the basic component of the English syllabus, takes the form of silent reading more often than reading aloud.

Extensive reading, on the other hand, is usually done at home for pleasure, or to acquire general information. It has a supplementary role in the process of learning a foreign language as it broadens the general knowledge of the learner and reinforces previously learned items. The material usually takes the form of short stories, novels, plays, poems, texts, magazines and journals. Common aspects of it include survey reading, superficial reading and skimming.

Silent Reading

Silent reading is reading for understanding or for comprehension. It is a very important skill that needs practising by pupils. This skill requires more teacher guidance and assistance in the early stages of learning the language. It should be introduced only after the new words and expressions have been learned.

The teacher is expected to help pupils develop their speed in silent reading. This can be realized by forming good habits such as the right sitting position, the proper distance between the page and the eyes, and the right eye movements to increase the span. The larger the span is, the faster reading can go. One way to attain such increase in eye span is to make pupils read a certain passage under pressure of time. Timing in silent reading increases the eye span to a great extent and makes pupils force themselves to read faster. The experienced teacher can estimate the time required for the pupils to go through the reading passage and for checking comprehension questions and language exercises. Comprehension questions should immediately follow silent reading. The questions should have a logical sequence. Furthermore they should involve an element of scanning and search reading. Such questions may be ranked from easy to difficult as follows:[1]

- Questions answerable by yes or no, or true or false.
- Information questions (who, what, where, when, how, how much, how many, how long) answerable by directly quoting from the passage.
- Questions (why or how) requiring the pupil to pull together several ideas from the passage.
- Inference questions that require the pupil to understand what the selection implies. That is, the information is not stated explicitly in the selection.
- Questions that require the pupil to form an opinion.

[1] These types of question follow Norris's classification 'Teaching Second Language Reading at the Advanced level: Goals, Techniques and procedures', TESOL Quarterly 4, No. 1 (March 1970), pp. 28–9.

The pupils should be able to answer without reference to the text. If, however, the text is difficult, they may be permitted to look in the book and get their answers from it. But pupils must be discouraged from becoming book-bound. The teacher may also encourage them to form their own questions about the passage. He must not allow them to write in Arabic or in English on the pages of their reading books, in order to keep the emphasis on the discourse and not on the equivalent meaning. Besides, direct translation should be avoided as far as possible. The foreign language (i.e. English) should be employed instead. This can be accomplished by resorting to synonyms, antonyms, simple definitions, restatement, circumlocution (saying in many words what may be said in few words) and even to gestures.

The words and expressions selected for special study should be written on the chalkboard, pronounced, explained and used in sentences by the teacher. Pupils may write them in their notebooks.

10.3 Reading Aloud

Reading aloud is another type of reading skill that can be utilized for certain purposes such as checking pupils' pronunciation, word stress, pauses, intonation and understanding. The passage to be read aloud should be short, complete and topical. Furthermore, the content and language of the text should be familiar and clear enough to be understood.

Training in oral reading stimulates the rapid association of sound–word concepts and affords practice in pronunciation and expression. Choral reading is recommended for improving pronunciation especially for pupils who are embarrassed when called upon to use the foreign language orally.

In conducting a reading aloud activity, the teacher is advised to consider the following points:

(a) Reading aloud comes only after pupils' silent reading, and after presenting and discussing new words, structures and expressions.

(b) While the books are closed, the pupils listen to the text recorded on a tape. This form may be called undivided model reading.

(c) After that, the teacher reads the passage sentence by sentence with pupils repeating after each sentence. This form is called divided model reading. It ensures more participation on the pupils' part because they read after their teacher instead of listening passively in the case of undivided model reading. Furthermore, this technique allows the best pronunciation, rhythm and intonation to be followed at once by the pupils.

(d) The next step is individual reading. Good pupils may start first so that they may provide examples for other classmates who will have a chance to read the passage.

(e) Reading round the class should be discouraged. A good teacher keeps the pupils always on the alert.

(f) To overcome passivity on the part of pupils, the teacher may ask them to correct mistakes made by the reader. This method encourages pupils to listen carefully and to follow up the reading.

(g) Individual pupils should not read the whole passage or for a long time. The opportunity should be given to others to participate.

(h) While reading, pupils should not be interrupted by questions about points in the passage. Questions may be asked at the end of the activity.

(i) Conversations or dialogue passages must not be read by one pupil. Such passages are to be dramatized. The teacher assigns a part or role to each pupil.

(j) Finally, the activity of reading aloud is not to be carried on for a long time in order to avoid boredom or sacrificing other more important language skills.

10.4 SQ 3R

This type of reading is more suitable for advanced students who benefit from this technique in retaining information. The term SQ 3R stands for 'Survey, Question, Read, Recite and Review', the five steps to be followed in technical reading.

1. *Survey*
Students survey the assigned pages in order to acquire a general idea of the material: its topic headings, sequence, assumptions, charts, questions, etc.

2. *Question*
After surveying, the student answers some questions based on the material he has just surveyed. These questions help him read with a purpose, looking for specific answers to get the information he has to focus on.

3. *Read*
The student reads as rapidly as possible because he knows what he is looking for, that is, seeking answers for the questions he has been set. While reading, he underlines the main ideas and key concepts.

4. *Recite*
At the end of each section, the student recites what he has read so as to check whether he can recall the material and to relate it to previous information.

5. *Review*
Finally, when the student has finished the assignment he reviews the material of the text to form a unified whole, and to check which parts he can recall and which parts he cannot. This also helps him to prepare for the next assignment.

10.5 Skimming

This type of reading is usually used when it is unnecessary to examine the text thoroughly. When we skim, for example, a newspaper or magazine, we just pass our eyes over headlines, titles, topic sentences and summaries. That is we are looking for the main idea of a passage. However, the skill is effective in improving the students' ability at getting information within a limited period of time.

Scanning is a variation of skimming. It refers to a quick overview of a passage for the sake of getting specific information. This type of reading occurs when using television listings/programmes, catalogues, telephone directories, etc.

Students may be asked to scan such material to solve whatever problem is presented. However, in pleasure reading we usually neither skim nor scan, but read for main ideas without paying close attention to details.

10.6 Supplementary Reading

Supplementary (or free) reading differs from both basic reading and reading comprehension in that it does not contain any (or at least only very few) words and structures which pupils have not met before. This reading activity aims at increasing the pupils' skill in the language and their command of words. It enriches their knowledge of the culture of the foreign people through introducing them to more mature and more timely material than that found in school textbooks. It also provides an opportunity for correlation with any special field in which the pupil is interested – science, sports, music, and so on. Because of these advantages, supplementary reading should be an inseparable part of the learning process. Encouraging pupils to read books and articles in the foreign language should form a part of regular EFL teaching from the elementary stages. It will be helpful if the teacher maintains a small library in the classroom or if the school library provides books. Pupils should be encouraged to keep a record of new words and expressions. A summary, oral or written, should be presented as evidence of the reading.

Supplementary reading is usually a grade less than the basic (or main) reader. This will encourage pupils to develop and maintain interest in free reading and help them revise and consolidate structures and words learnt in previous years.

To conduct a successful supplementary reading lesson, the teacher may follow these procedures:

1. The teacher gives pupils a general idea of the story's setting (e.g. time, era, way of life, the author, place of incidents, etc.) in order to arouse their interest and curiosity.

2. If the teacher finds it necessary to provide a brief outline of the main topic of the story, he may do that to motivate the pupils to read the whole book. The important factor is that the pupils should enjoy what they read.

3. The first chapter of the story is to be read and discussed in class to familiarize the pupils with the author's style, language used, characters of the story, and the like.

4. The next step can be an assignment. At the beginning, just a few pages are to be assigned, and as pupils progress in the story, the assignment can be increased. The teacher may give the class some questions about the part to be read at home. These questions are to be discussed in detail in the following lessons. This technique would compel pupils to read the required chapter or section. It would also encourage them to look up new words in the dictionary.

5. In the next lesson the teacher checks whether the reading of the required part has been done; then discussion on the part read starts.

6. Selected passages or paragraphs of special interest can be read silently unless there is a need for oral reading. However, reading the whole of any

text aloud in class is time-consuming and will prevent pupils from learning to read fast. Following this procedure may result in boredom. The only exception is the play or a dialogue which is meant to be dramatized as a classroom activity.

Whether the reading activity is silent or aloud, comprehension questions should follow.

7. To prompt pupils to read, the teacher may write a few questions on the blackboard before the class starts reading; then he calls on pupils to find out the answers for these questions as soon as they can.

8. Pupils should be encouraged to comment critically on the characters or incidents in the story and to conduct discussion. The conversation should be brisk and lively and should give every opportunity for the greatest number of pupils to take part. Minor errors may be overlooked to help pupils gain confidence in their ability to express themselves in English. All pupils must be encouraged to participate in the discussion.

9. The teacher must draw the pupils' attention to important incidents and sections that matter in order to keep a sense of continuity in the story as a whole.

10. At the end of the lesson, the teacher gives a new homework assignment on the next part to be discussed, and the process will be repeated as before.

10.7

Reading Stages

Reading is a development process which goes through several stages starting from words and phrases to advanced reading and communication practice. The FL teacher must have authentic reading materials for all these stages to help pupils develop their reading efficiency.

Stage One: Word Level

At the word level, the concern is with the association of form and sound symbol, spelling and sound – regular or irregular. Pupils should spend enough time on sound–symbol correspondence. Flash cards are useful in recognizing shapes (single letters and common digraphs) and associating the proper sounds with the shapes, turning them into words.

When using flash cards, the teacher first says the sound-name which pupils repeat. He, then, shows the card and repeats its sound. The class repeat as groups and as individuals. The word is tested by showing any card for a short time until some pupils say the right sound. The teacher repeats the sound, and class or groups repeat after him.

Stage Two: Sentence Level

At this level, the teacher gives pupils practice in patterns of high frequency. Subsequently they may read sentences developed from dialogue material familiar to them, for the sake of meaning intonation and stress. The tape-recorder helps in this respect. The teacher must see if the pupils are repeating meaningful segments. Word reading should also continue and the importance of reading vocabulary should be stressed. The pupils should be given preparation for close passage reading. Words and structures must be familiar to pupils.

The following activities provide techniques for teaching reading at this stage:

1. Asking pupils to read sentences with words they already know. This can be practised by cue cards (i.e. cards with a word on each), which pupils place in the desired order, e.g.: a model sentence, an answer to a question, etc.

2. The teacher writes sentences on the chalkboard or on overhead transparencies for pupils to read.

3. Pupils may practise reading sentences in the class or in the language laboratory or with cassette/tape-recorder, etc.

4. Songs are an excellent technique for improving pupils' pronunciation, rhythm and stress. They create pleasure in the classroom and stimulate the learning of the foreign language. Moreover they offer a pleasant way of practising or reviewing vocabulary.

Stage Three: Paragraph Level

At this stage pupils are introduced to simple narrative or conversational material. Passages should not exceed one printed page. This is done under the guidance of the teacher who often uses the materials provided in the textbook. However, additional selections can be used for guided reading practice.

For reading practice, at this stage, the teacher may prepare duplicated sheets of texts which pupils read, or use overhead transparencies on which he writes reading selections. This technique is effective as the teacher controls what the pupils are reading. He can thus watch their eye movements, or mask certain parts of the passage, or point out certain words, functions and phrases. Pupils can practise guided reading individually, in pairs or in small groups. He may correct reading errors immediately, or the pupils correct themselves.

The following are some reading activities which are suitable for this stage:

1. Reading for structure signals. The teacher draws the pupils' attention to written grammar signals.

2. Techniques of inference. The teacher guides pupils to infer meanings or simple conclusions from paragraph context.

3. Techniques of paraphrase. With this technique pupils try to grasp the meaning of a selection in its entirety.

4. Reading for information. This involves three levels of reading practice:
   (a) the beginning level with questions that require restatement of the text;
   (b) the intermediate level with content questions that require the pupils to demonstrate their understanding of the entire texts;
   (c) the advanced level with questions initiated by pupils who also provide the answers to their own questions and suggest a suitable title for the whole passage.

Stage Four: Reading Longer Selections

As pupils progress in learning the language needed for reading, they should read longer selections in addition to guided reading passages. That is, pupils' reading activities may be classed as intensive and extensive. The former is what they have in the text reader or course book, whereas extensive reading is meant for enjoyment, for general information. Pupils should be offered a choice of readings and select topics which interest them. They may also be asked to give a summary or an outline of what they are reading or to rewrite the selection by changing some of the nouns, adjectives, tenses and direct speech. They could then present their version to the others in the class.

Stage Five: Individualized Reading

This is the advanced stage of reading. Students are given the freedom to select from a list of available material what they wish to read. Students depend on themselves in reading as they feel confident enough to pick up a book or a newspaper and read it for their own pleasure and enlightenment.

Nevertheless, the teacher's guidance is generally needed. The teacher may provide the class with a list of readings from different fields of knowledge: art, science, literature, and so on. The teacher classifies the readings in categories from easy to advanced with a synopsis of each reading.

Students review the list and read the synopsis before they make a selection. After that they check their choice with the teacher who either approves of the selection, depending on the level of difficulty and appropriateness of the subject or suggests alternatives.

After finishing the selection, a student makes a note of this in the notebook he keeps for this purpose. To motivate students, the teacher may ask content questions to ensure understanding of the selection, and may give marks for high achievement.

10.8 Communicative Practice

Reading practice can be made part of a process of communication if pupils are given the opportunity to react directly to it by expressing their personal opinions. This can be realized as follows:

(a) Selection of reading materials

Pupils may be involved in the selection of reading materials. One way of doing this is through a group discussion. They discuss problems related to their interests, hopes and goals. After discussion, they report their ideas to the teacher. The teacher records their comments and from the list of their interests he selects appropriate readings. Thus the pupils are participating actively in the selection of reading material and in the creation of a piece of discourse.

(b) Purposive reading skills

A pupil reads a given text if he feels that what he gets out of it will fill an information gap. Such a need will improve pupils' reading proficiency as they acquire the strategies of scanning and search reading.

However, pupils should be instructed how to scan the text and how to reject the irrelevant parts so as to identify the required information.

(c) Question formation

Pupils should be given the chance to write questions about the text after reading it. This makes them look closely at the text and improves their comprehension. After writing the questions, the teacher divides the class into pairs or small groups to discuss the questions and their answers. For example pupil A puts questions to pupil B who responds without referring to the text unless there is a point of disagreement. When pupil A finishes his questions, pupil B becomes the questioner, and so on.

(d) Pupils' writings as reading materials

Pupils may be asked to write on a certain topic, or to prepare an interview or to write about a visit to a museum, etc. When they return to school, they read what they have written to the teacher.

(e) Discourse analysis

This technique requires careful and close reading on the part of pupils as they will examine the writer's organization of the text and how the ideas are arranged. For example, they might be asked to identify topic sentences, clues that signal relationships between sentences, paragraphs and ideas. Working together in small groups will help pupils to interact with each other.

(f) Supplementary readers

These are simplified or abridged selections, often used to develop speed and ease of reading. They are usually read at leisure and mainly for enjoyment. The teacher can make use of them for communicative practice. One technique of doing so is as follows:
1. The teacher provides the class with simplified readers on different topics, to read at home.
2. Each pupil selects a book and takes it home to read within a limited period of time.
3. The teacher assigns a day for group discussions and divides the class into groups of three pupils.
4. One pupil talks for five minutes about his book, then the other two question him for another five minutes.
5. The same process is followed with the other two pupils. Each pupil has a total of ten minutes.
6. The complete exercise takes thirty minutes, and the remaining fifteen minutes of the lesson are set aside for the teacher's feedback.

In such a technique, reading activities become pupil-centred. The pupils select the readings, ask each other questions and express their opinions.

(g) Questionnaires and self-tests

Other ways of communicative practice are personal questionnaires or self-tests which are frequently published in popular magazines or journals. In such exercises, pupils read, and respond to specific questions about themselves. They give their opinions or personal priorities. In using such techniques, the focus is on the reading and comprehension. The pupils need to understand the given questions before answering them appropriately.

Most of the above reading activities should be conducted in group work. This enables pupils to interact with each other easily and freely with minimum interference from the teacher. In addition, it gives them the opportunity to learn. The size of the groups should be appropriate, preferably four pupils of mixed abilities in each group. The group leader coordinates the task and sees that everyone in the group talks (in English), all questions are solved and a consensus is reached.

10.9
Planning a Reading Lesson (Procedures for Intensive Reading)

The plan of a reading lesson may contain the following sequence:

1. The teacher writes on the chalkboard the day and date, lesson number, part number, and page.

2. The teacher motivates the class by reviewing the material of the previous lesson regarding content, vocabulary, patterns, spelling and other language components.

3. The teacher presents some of the new words and structures that will appear in the section he has planned to teach.

4. The teacher tries to arouse the pupils' interest in the reading. Thus, if the reading is part of a longer story, he should relate it to the whole story. If the lesson is new, he should brief the class on the main theme, and so on. If there is a picture, he can ask pupils questions about it. The more interesting the teacher can make the reading topic, the easier it will be to read.

5. Now the pupils are ready to read the passage silently.

6. After silent reading, the teacher asks a few comprehension questions on the passage content to evaluate their ability to comprehend what they have read.

7. The next step is model reading. The teacher can read the passage aloud with pupils listening or repeating to give them an example they should imitate. The teacher may use taped material recorded by native speakers of English.

8. After model reading, pupils may read the passage aloud and individually. The teacher, however, should not overuse reading aloud as the usefulness of this skill is limited. Its main function is to practise special pronunciation problems.

9. The class may then do some of the exercises on words or patterns usually included in the reading textbook.

10. The lesson ends with the teacher assigning new homework on material done orally in the class.

These steps are systematic but the teacher is free to omit some of them if time does not allow him to do all of them, or if he wants to emphasize certain points.

In addition to the above procedures, the teacher may:

(a) clarify the purpose of the reading passage;
(b) highlight language functions and their context in the passage;
(c) help pupils read words in logical groups, that is, small groups of words which make sense;
(d) help pupils to guess the meaning of words from context;
(e) if time allows, do a paragraph-by-paragraph analysis, i.e. engage pupils in discourse analysis.

Chapter Eleven

Teaching Writing

Introduction

Writing is an active means of communicating ideas. In its functional sense, it is equated with speech since both are concerned with conveying information. Thus a pupil practises in writing what he has practised orally, and expresses through it what he understands and wishes to convey. While oral practice is necessary to become fluent in speaking a language, practice is a prerequisite to mastering the skill of writing. However, errors are more tolerated in speaking than in writing.

In addition to its communicative function, writing is a major classroom procedure, an important language activity (e.g. dictation, composition, summary making, written exercises, tests, etc.), and an effective technique to reinforce the oral and written language material. It also provides evidence of pupils' achievements, and a source for later reference.

Writing is considered a significant language skill that should be developed at an early stage of learning the foreign language. It requires the following:

(a) A knowledge of the English alphabet so that pupils can learn how to spell and how to identify letters in print.

(b) An understanding of the orthographic system, i.e. the relationship between sounds and written symbols. That is, pupils must learn control of the graphic symbols that represent the sounds of the language.

(c) A knowledge of the mechanics of writing: spelling, capitalization, punctuation, paragraph indentation, leaving spaces between words, syllable division, and other writing conventions.

(d) A knowledge of possible sentence structures in English.

(e) Familiarity with grammatical, referential or anaphoric connectors.

(f) Familiarity with lexical connectors, e.g. repetition of key words or the same word in a different form (deciding/decision), or the use of synonyms and antonyms, etc.

(g) Skill in sentence-combining to create an effective paragraph, and a knowledge of the organization of the whole composition.

(h) Familiarity with transitional words or phrases such as:
- (i)   Addition: e.g. and, furthermore, also;
- (ii)   Comparison: e.g. likewise, similarly;
- (iii)   Result: e.g. accordingly, hence, therefore, etc.;
- (iv)   Contrast and concession: e.g. but, although, even if, whereas, however;
- (v)   Passage of time: e.g. at least, afterwards, then, etc;
- (vi)   Enumeration: e.g. first, second, finally, etc.;
- (vii)   Example: e.g. for example, in other words, namely, etc.;
- (viii) Summary: e.g. in brief, in conclusion, etc.

(i) Adequate control of syntax and vocabulary in order to put ideas into writing.

(j) Some experience of listening, speaking and reading.

The ability to write well grows out of these integrated skills, as will be seen in the following sections.

However, learning to write is a gradual process which begins with simple copying and ends with free expression. Pupils should be trained systematically, under the guidance of the teacher, through several stages of writing experience, namely: handwriting, copying dictation, controlled, guided and free writing. Such gradation is necessary for developing, logically and cumulatively, the writing skill. Thus, we cannot teach pupils to write a paragraph before teaching them how to write a sentence. That is, the mastery at one level is necessary before the pupils proceed to the next level. For pedagogical purposes the writing programme will be divided into three main stages: controlled writing, guided writing and free writing. They will be discussed separately with the procedures and techniques of teaching each of them.

11.1

Controlled Writing

The first stage of the writing skill includes handwriting, copying (or transcription), dictation and spelling. These aspects of writing are completely controlled by the teacher. Their main function is to teach pupils the mechanics of writing accuracy and readiness for further writing activities. For this purpose they should be practised systematically and frequently especially at the initial stages of learning English in order to foster good habits of writing.

Handwriting

This skill is the first writing activity. It is a form of imitative writing in which pupils learn how to write the alphabet and familiar words of specific significance. Pupils start the activity with strokes like these: | | |, ///, -----, etc; then with straight line letters such as: i, l, v, w, x etc. After that, they proceed to practise curved-line letters, such as s and c; then they write combined letters composed of straight and curved lines such as b, B, d, D, p and q. To ensure the initiation of correct habits in writing, the first written work is to be done on four parallel lines; later on, they write on two lines and eventually on one line as their ability develops.

The teacher, while training pupils in handwriting, must take into consideration the following points:

1. He must show young learners how to hold the pen or pencil properly, and how to sit in the correct manner with the copybook in front of them in the right position. If the teacher has left them without observation or guidance, they may develop bad habits of writing which will be reflected in their later writing activities.

2. The teacher then has to show pupils the manner of writing, and the formation of letters and words. The pupils must write from left to right on straight horizontal lines and from the model at the top of the page. The size of letters must be unified: all small letters should be of the same size as well as capital letters, and all should be written with the same slant and with equal spaces between them. Later, pupils should be trained to write cursively.

3. Initial handwriting drills are to be written in pencil, and not in ink, because beginners usually make many mistakes, and they can erase them and thus keep the handwriting copybook neat and tidy.

4. The teacher should write a model on the blackboard in order to show pupils the direction of letter formation.

5. After that he has to go round the pupils to check the manual movement which is the main purpose of this activity. The teacher must not consider the handwriting period as a rest time for him, nor should he devote much class time to it at the expense of other language activities. He has to make the activity interesting and purposeful.

Copying: (Transcription)

This phase of writing skill is usually assigned or practised as soon as the pupils can write with ease the letters and the combinations of letters for the words or phrases they have already mastered. That is to say, the material meant for copying should be familiar to the pupils because the purposes of this activity are:

(a) to reinforce previously learned words and patterns;
(b) to develop young learners' consciousness of spelling and to fix the correct written forms in their minds;
(c) to draw pupils' attention to punctuation marks;
(d) to train pupils further in handwriting.

The material for transcription can be taken from the reading passages that have been studied. This material should be short and form a coherent context so as to avoid boredom and mechanical copying. At the beginning, the teacher may give pupils two or three sentences; then, as they gain experience with the language, he may increase the copying assignment accordingly. Short dialogues and substitution drills are good exercises for this activity which should be practised frequently especially at the initial stages of learning English.

The following activities are examples of effective techniques that can maintain pupils' interest in copying.

1. Fill in the blanks:
   In this technique pupils fill in the blanks by copying model sentences in

their classwork copybooks or on duplicated sheets.

Example: I am so glad you could pass the test.

I –– s– gl–– –ou c–––d p––– th– t––t

2. Scrambled sentences:

Pupils are asked to rearrange given words presented in random order to as to make correct meaningful sentences. Example: the book/bought/ Ali/yesterday/.

3. Putting sentences in correct order:

Pupils rewrite a set of sentences in the correct order so as to make a simple discourse or a short dialogue. Example:

I'm going fishing.

May I come with you?

Where are you going, Ali?

4. Magazine pictures:

The teacher brings to the class magazine pictures or draws figures on the board, or puts pictures in the projector, then he asks pupils to write corresponding lines of dialogue.

5. Matching questions and answers:

In this technique pupils copy questions and their appropriate responses. Example:

Where are you going?

How are you?

When do you go to bed?

How old are you?

What time do you go to school?

About ten o'clock.

Very well, thank you.

At seven thirty (7.30).

I'm 14 years old.

Home.

6. Correcting sentences:

The pupils change the sentences by adding yesterday/tomorrow or the point of view, or the subject or the gender of the subject, etc.

7. Sentence building:

Pupils are given linguisitic forms on a chart and are asked to select the components that may correctly be used together in order to create sentences. Example:

I		Arabic
Ali	spoke	orange juice
She	took	maths
They		tickets
Ali and Laila	studied	milk
You		English
Laila and I	bought	tea
		a radio

8. Crossword puzzles:
   Pupils fill in crossword puzzles with given words that go with their standard of English.

9. Sentence completion:
   Pupils are given a set of related sentences with some deleted words in each: then they are asked to fill in the missing words. The teacher may provide the required words, depending on the nature of the sentences.

Dictation

After there has been sufficient practice in imitative writing (handwriting and copying), the next step is dictation. This type of writing skill is an essential activity for the development of spelling consciousness in learners, so it should be given at frequent intervals. Dictation is, however, more difficult than copying because the pupil here uses the mind's eye with which he visualizes the spelling of a word and English spelling does not always correspond with the sound (e.g. know, through, enough, right, write, etc.). Dictation material should be brief, familiar and not beyond the pupils' range of comprehension. If dictation is presented properly, it will be a valuable instrument by which pupils can practise other aspects of language learning such as aural comprehension, distinguishing sounds and words, comprehending the meaning of a passage, and recognizing grammatical forms and accuracy.

Procedures for giving dictation

In the early stages of spelling, pupils are usually given words or simple patterns chosen from their main readers. The following exercises can be helpful:

1. Look at the pictures and fill in the missing letters:
   (a) --n   (drawing: sun)
   (b) t--l-   (drawing: table)
   (c) k-i--   (drawing: knife) etc.

2. Look at the pictures and re-arrange the following letters to make words:
   (a) fsih   (drawing: fish)
   (b) wtcah   (drawing: watch)
   (c) btotel   (drawing: bottle)

3. Look at the pictures and give the English words:
   (a) _____ (drawing: cup)
   (b) _____ (drawing: chair)
   (c) _____ (drawing: plane) etc.

4. Look at each picture and choose the word that goes with it:
   (a) dog   mouse   cat   (drawing: mouse)
   (b) apple   banana   egg   (drawing: apple)
   (c) happy   smiling   unhappy   (drawing: unhappy face)

5. Re-arrange the letters of the following words. The explanation beside each word will help you:
   (a) hscar: (   ) a loud noise
   (b) ptmey: (   ) the opposite of full
   (c) sialro: (   ) a man who works on a ship, etc.

6. Write the full forms of the following abbreviations:
   (a) lab. = laboratory
   (b) 1st = first
   (c) st. = street, etc.

7. Combine the following:
   (a) swim + ing = swimming
   (b) monkey + s = monkeys
   (c) knife + s   = knives
   (d) study + d   = studied, etc.

8. Full dictation:
   The teacher dictates sentences which the pupils write out.

Gradually these varieties are expanded to more complex ones. At a later stage pupils can be given a short paragraph, a dialogue or a passage selected from the textbook. The procedure for this goes as follows:

1. The teacher assigns the passage to be prepared at home for dictation.

2. At the next session the teacher reads the whole passage while pupils listen without writing anything. The reading should be normally paced, clear and expressive.

3. The teacher dictates the assigned passage to his class. He dictates in units like these: His son Ali/did not get a car/until last year. Each sentence has to be repeated twice at a fairly slow speed.

4. Punctuation marks should be dictated.

5. Difficult words can be written on the blackboard.

6. When the dictation finishes, the teacher reads the passage once more.

7. Immediately after that correction starts. Each pupil may check his own work or exchange his copybook with his neighbour. Correction should be done in red ink. This technique of self-correction saves the teacher's time and secures instant feedback. The teacher, however, has to collect the dictation copybooks once a month to check pupils' correction.

8. Pupils are required to write their mis-spelled words in the correct forms three times each.

9. The teacher summarizes the most common errors made and discusses them with the class, giving suggestions for avoiding them in future.

To help pupils improve their spelling, the teacher may provide them with some suitable generalizations which can help in developing their ability to spell correctly. Examples of these generalizations are: forms of plurals of nouns, of numbers, of letters, of words ending in 'y', doubling final consonant, suffixes, combinations and abbreviations. All these exercises have proved to be very helpful.

11.2

Guided Writing

The second stage of teaching writing involves two graded steps of composition writing, namely controlled composition/directed composition and semi-controlled/guided composition.

The principle of these aspects of composition writing is to provide graded guidance in vocabulary and structures so that pupils will not make many mistakes.

Controlled composition

In controlled writing, pupils are usually provided with the needed keywords and expressions or a model of some type with directions for manipulation in rewriting the model. The aim of this is to ensure that what pupils write is grammatically correct. This activity of controlled writing may take any of the following forms:

1. Missing Words

A passage or isolated sentences are given with some deleted words. The task is to supply the missing items. Examples:
(a) Fill in the blanks (with cued words in parentheses)

(look) I _____ at our playground. I can see Ali and Omar.

(run, sit) Ali _____ but Omar _____ .

(enjoy) They _____ themselves.

(b) This is our classroom. There _____ four walls and _____ (number) windows. There _____ one door. There _____ one blackboard. There _____ (number) students in the room. There _____ a teacher. He _____ sitting at his desk. He _____ teaching us. We _____ learning English.

2. Word Ordering

A group of jumbled words is given to pupils who are to re-arrange them to make a complete sentence, e.g. speak, he, French, can, fluently. He can speak French fluently, or Can he speak French fluently?

3. Re-arrangement of sentences

In this exercise a group of jumbled sentences is given. Pupils re-arrange them logically to build up a complete paragraph. Example:

Re-arrange the following sentences to build up a good paragraph. (The first and last sentences are in their right order.)
1. Many centuries ago a man lived in Spain.
2. He climbed a mountain and jumped in the air.
3. He made two wings and put them on his body.
4. Then he believed he could fly like a bird.
5. But he forgot to put a tail on his back.
6. He looked at the birds for a long time.
7. So, he fell down and was badly hurt.

In answering this, the sentences may be put in this order:
$1+6+4+3+5+2+7$.

4. Imitation of specific patterns

In this activity, the teacher gives the class a model sentence and a group of substitutes which are to be patterned after the model. Example:

The model sentence: Ali cleans the car every day.

Substitutes: Fatima, house, morning.
Parallel sentences: Fatima cleans the house every morning.
Alternative forms often require the selection of the appropriate pronouns, verb tense, subject–verb concord, and the like.
Example:

Model sentence: The pupils walk to the class with books in their hands.
Substitutes: girl, go, home, bag.
Parallel sentence: The girl goes home with a bag in her hand.

5. *Parallel paragraph*

In this exercise, a model paragraph is given with directions for rewriting it by employing specific language manipulations. Pupils substitute some words in the model paragraph for others to get a new paragraph grammatically parallel to the given one. In the beginning, pupils should be provided with simple short passages based on their interests, knowledge and experience. It is important that pupils write about something familiar and interesting to them. Variations on writing activity are multiple substitution exercises or conversions. Pupils either change or expand the structural patterns of the model passage which serves to suggest content and ideas. Change can be achieved in the following ways:

(a) Change the subject.
(b) Change the subject and verb to the plural or vice-versa.
(c) Change by adding yesterday, tomorrow, now, etc.
(d) Change the point of view of the paragraph, affirmative to negative and the opposite.

6. *Sentence expansion*

In this activity, the model paragraph is given with numbers inserted in the sentences. Some modifiers are also supplied. Pupils are asked to rewrite the paragraph by inserting an appropriate modifier in place of each of the numbers. Example:

The (1) teacher walked (2) to the (3) class with a number of (4) books in his (5) hand. As he entered the classroom, the pupils were talking (6) but he smiled (7) and greeted them.

1. old, English, history, unpopular
2. quickly, confidently, slowly, impatiently
3. big, noisy, quiet, happy
4. English, thick, coloured, folded
5. shaking, right, outstretched, tied up
6. softly, quietly, loudly
7. pleasantly, attractively, in a friendly manner

The pupil selects a suitable expression for each of the numbers.

7. *Sentence completion*

In this exercise a part of a sentence or phrase is omitted and the pupils are required to supply the missing part. Guidance for writing should still be provided so that pupils can add the correct and proper forms. Example:
Directions: Ali is a young artist. He is riding a bus on his way to an interview

for a job in T.V. He is excited. First he takes the wrong bus, then the right one. Here is the dialogue between him and the first bus conductor. Fill in the missing part of the dialogue.

Conductor : Fares, please. Where _____?
Ali : To Amman Street, please.
Conductor : You are on the wrong bus.
We don't go _____.
Ali : _____ you? I thought _____ _____ the _____ bus.
Conductor : No. This is a 23. You want bus number 18.
Ali : _____ one? Where _____ _____ _____ one?
Conductor : Get off at the _____ _____ _____.
(He gets into the 18 at the next bus-stop), etc.

8. Guided writing using pictures

In this writing activity, the teacher shows the class a large picture or wall-chart. He gives any necessary vocabulary or structures. Then he asks pupils to write about it, or he may ask questions about things or objects in the picture in order to elicit a series of statements that will form a composition.

9. Dicto-Comp

Another type of controlled writing is dicto-comp. This activity involves two aspects of writing skill. The first one is dictation and its function is to check the accuracy of spelling and punctuation, while the other is text reconstruction. The procedure for this activity goes like this: the teacher reads a short passage of some interest or tells the class an interesting story. After that he asks some questions about the content of the material and he gives some cue words to help pupils recall the incidents. Then he asks them to rewrite the material previously read.

10. Sentence-combining exercises

The teacher, in this writing activity, gives the pupils a group of simple sentences (with or without connectors), and then asks them to combine them into more complex ones to form a paragraph or so. Here is an example:

Ali returned home from school at 2 o'clock yesterday. He read the newspaper. He had dinner with his family. After dinner, he sat with his children in the garden. The garden is beautiful and shady. He has two children. Their names are Sameer and Laila. They are too young to go to school. They have good friends. They play with them.

One possible way of joining these simple sentences into more complex ones is the following:

When Ali returned home from school at 2 o'clock yesterday, he read the newspaper and had dinner with his family. Then he sat with his children, Sameer and Laila, in their beautiful and shady garden. The children are too young to go to school, but they have good friends to play with.

When drilling such exercises, pupils may try various combinations, or change the tenses, or change the names of the persons or pronouns, etc.

The foregoing exercises in controlled composition are not exhaustive. A competent English language teacher can devise or adapt other exercises. It is preferable, however, to base the exercises on materials that have been previously read or learned by pupils.

Semi-controlled composition

The second type of guided writing is semi-controlled composition which is an important step in moving from controlled to free composition. At the previous stage, pupils were manipulating language using new words and topics provided by the teacher. Now the control is relaxed and pupils can add specific ideas or constructions to their composition. However, there is still some structural control or guidance in order to develop the ability to write correct English. Suggestions regarding the content or form of what pupils should write are also given. Exercises used at this stage include:

1. Written interviews, real or imaginary

There are different types of interview assignment. One technique is for pupils to conduct interviews with friends or with teachers. Pupils can pretend they are interviewing famous people, football players, and the like. The teacher may give the class some key words, directions and a few lines which can stimulate pupils to develop the dialogue.

2. Pictorial exercises

The teacher gives the class a series of pictures or film strips. The pupils are asked to write about the content or the sequence of events in these pictures, guided by the teacher's questions or discussion.

3. Narrative exercises

The teacher reads a story or an event. He writes some leading questions on the chalkboard. The pupils' task is to retell the story in written form, or to summarize it.

4. Short story completion

In this activity pupils may complete a dialogue of which the first few lines are given, or write an ending to a story by using their imagination. Example:

The family were sitting in the living room, watching a favourite programme on the T.V. when they heard a strange movement in the house. The children got afraid and started to cry but the mother hushed them. The father turned off the television and went to see what was going on. Suddenly he saw a strange face looking through the window. The father shouted 'Who is it?' (It was a stranger who lost his way and came to the house to . . .)

As a variation of this exercise the teacher presents the class with appropriate outlines or key words of a story whose theme is also given; then he asks the pupils to write a new story.

5. Letter writing

In this activity, the teacher reads a letter of some interest. He also shows the method of writing letters (writing address, salutations and ending), gives some key words or expressions and the theme of the reply. Pupils write a letter on the basis of the information provided.

At this stage, the letters should be personal or friendly. Most pupils have friends or relatives who live abroad. They can write about events of home life, about things they know or care about, and so on.

6. Cued dialogue
The teacher writes on the board some brief cues for a dialogue. Pupils write out the complete conversation.

7. Cloze exercises
The teacher gives pupils a passage in which some words are deleted. The pupils fill in the missing words.

8. Changing spoken to written English
The teacher gives the pupils a transcript of spoken English and asks them to change it into a piece of formal writing.

9. Changing a narrative to a dialogue, or a dialogue to a narrative

10. Writing an account or a report on a written article or a book

11. Writing a summary or an outline of material which pupils have read
There are other forms of guided writing such as answering a series of questions about a person or event, note-taking from a lecture or talk and integrated composition, i.e. writing a composition subject based on a comprehension passage, and so on.

Procedures of guided composition
There are various procedures and techniques for teaching controlled or semi-controlled composition. Some exercises lend themselves to group activity while others require pupils to work on individual assignments. The following steps constitute the basic procedures which the teacher may follow in teaching guided composition:

1. The teacher must make sure that the pupils understand the model he presents. This may require explanation of some words or structures.
2. Pupils must be encouraged to ask questions if they are not certain of the correct response so as to avoid making mistakes.
3. It is important that the pupils receive feedback as soon as possible on their writing.
4. Mistakes should be indicated by underlining. The teacher can indicate the different types of mistake by writing the following abbreviations or symbols in the margin: sp = spelling; S–V = subject–verb agreement; prep = wrong preposition; tns = wrong tense; ¶ = new paragraph, WW = wrong word; neg = wrong negative form, etc.
5. Mistakes should be corrected by pupils themselves. This may require re-writing the composition in its correct form.
6. The teacher after correcting the compositions should discuss common mistakes with the class. This is part of the teaching process which leads to re-learning.

11.3

Free Writing

This stage involves free composition. Pupils having practised controlled and guided composition, are now able to manipulate language with some originality of thought and freedom from common errors.

This activity requires adequate preparation. Thus, the teacher must instruct pupils in the mechanics of free composition such as: the date, adequate margins, the title (correctly-capitalized), indentation (leaving an inch-wide space at the beginning of each paragraph) and clear handwriting. The teacher must teach them the qualities of a good paragraph such as (a) unity (the unity of thought in all sentences within a paragraph); (b) coherence (the linking of sentences); (c) emphasis (the ordering of sentences and ideas); (d) clarity (the elimination of ambiguities to show relationship and progress of thought) and, (e) correctness (careful use of vocabulary, correct spelling and punctuation, good use of grammatical structures and a good conclusion that draws the paragraph together). To train pupils to build up a long composition effectively, the teacher may analyse some models of composition to show the class the unity and coherence of all the paragraphs.

As for the topic, the teacher has to present the class with a subject that is either of particular significance to them or that lends itself to facility of expression. That is, the topic should be meaningful and interesting to the pupils, or else composition classes will be boring. It is advised to start with descriptive and narrative topics or letter-writing, and later on expository writing or essay-writing.

Adequate planning for the composition lesson requires the teacher to follow these steps: preparation, writing, correction, and re-learning.

Preparation

In preparation for a composition, the teacher introduces the subject the pupils are going to write about, clarifies any difficulties in it and writes necessary outlines or vocabulary and expressions related to the subject. This presentation may take the form of a short oral introduction, or of showing the class pictures, slides or even a film.

The teacher, then, conducts a discussion with the class. This provides the pupils with a good opportunity to communicate facts and ideas from their own experience, to express themselves freely and to use English in a realistic context. At the same time, the discussion is useful for the teacher to get acquainted with some of the language problems of the pupils so that he can remedy them in due time. Before the discussion starts, the teacher writes an outline on the blackboard to stimulate pupils on the subject. Then taking the points on the outline one at a time, he calls on individual pupils to give information about the particular point. And by encouraging the rest of the class to ask further questions (to get more information), or to make additional comments, the teacher can engage the whole class in a lively discussion on the target subject. Another possibility is to organize the class into 'buzz' groups of four or five pupils for further discussion of the outline in order to allow for more oral preparation.

The teacher then takes up the next point on the outline and discusses it with the class in the same way as he did with the first one, and so on until all the points are covered. The pupils, while discussing the subject, can write the words, expressions or structures that have been brought out by the discussion and that may appear in the composition they are going to write. However, the teacher should direct them to select the most relevant items to the subject.

When the discussion is finished, the teacher gives assignment for the next composition lesson. He asks pupils to prepare a rough draft of a composition on the subject they have discussed orally. If they have shown interest in the subject he may direct them to other sources where they can gather more information. Pupils may consult appropriate books and newspapers, or they can discuss with friends and family members.

Writing

On the next day of the composition lesson, pupils will be ready to begin writing. It is desirable to have them write their composition in the classroom, under the supervision of the teacher. They may write a rough draft at home, but the final copy should be written in class. This is to ensure that they write from their own knowledge and are not tempted to copy the information from outside sources such as parents, relatives or friends who may do the writing for them. While they are writing, the teacher moves about the room to give individual help where needed but he must be careful not to distract the pupils' concentration.

Correcting compositions

In correcting pupils' compositions, the teacher may correct all mistakes, or select some of them. He may also circle those errors that he feels they can correct themselves because the correct forms were given during the discussion stage. The teacher should refrain from writing the correct alternative forms. Instead of writing corrected items on the pupils' papers, he may use abbreviations or symbols characterizing different types of errors. There are many symbols, and every teacher can develop his own correction symbols and give them to his pupils at the beginning of the course.

When correcting composition, the teacher must also indicate features that lead to ambiguity, redundancy in expression, incoherence or lack of sequence and subject development. These are important in writing creatively.

Re-learning

The final step in the procedure of composition writing is the reinforcing or re-teaching process. Thus, after correcting and returning the compositions, the teacher reviews with the class the common mistakes he has come across. Bad compositions as well as good ones are to be discussed and analysed. This will provide pupils with feedback on their writing. To reinforce some grammatical constructions or other items involved in the writing of the composition, the teacher may give the class exercises (oral or written) with the purpose of re-teaching. Pupils are required to correct mistakes pointed out by the teacher and the teacher should make sure that the pupils check their compositions.

Part Five

Procedures
and
Techniques

Introduction

This part focuses on some practical aspects that make the process of teaching and learning more effective and communicatively orientated, and help in sustaining pupils' motivation.

They are lesson planning, classroom procedures, teaching aids, the importance of motivation and language testing and will be discussed in detail in the following chapters.

Chapter Twelve

Lesson Planning

Introduction

Careful planning of lessons is a prerequisite of efficient teaching. When a lesson is well prepared, the teacher gets more satisfaction from his work. In addition, it creates interest in the material and a desire to learn on the part of pupils who respond and understand the lesson more readily. The teacher must know the steps he follows, and what behaviour is expected from the pupils throughout the lesson. This requires identification of the educational aims of each lesson, the learning activities to attain these aims, the strategies of instruction to be employed and the aids to be used. Moreover he must familiarize himself with the instructional materials he is required to utilize in his teaching. He should also decide in advance which aspects of the unit are to be given more emphasis and what degree of proficiency the pupils must develop with respect to each of these aspects. The teacher thus must not leave things to chance or guesswork. The lesson plan ought to be comprehensive and motivating. It must cater for the needs of the pupils, their interests, age, background and abilities. Other factors to be taken into consideration are the size of the class and the physical classroom set-up. In sum, teaching is best when the teacher is able to draw up his lesson plans according to the needs, interests and capacities of the pupils involved.

12.1

Characteristics of Good Planning

Lesson planning varies according to the subject the teacher intends to teach. Some subjects may necessitate detailed plans while others require a brief outline. However, it often happens that a certain activity takes longer than anticipated. The teacher has to make some changes or modifications in the lesson plan. The same applies when an activity fails to interest the class. A well constructed plan should include provisions for the beginning, the middle and the end of the lesson.

At the beginning of a lesson, the teacher must find some means of eliciting pupils' interest. Although there are no fixed procedures about how a lesson should proceed, an experienced teacher can employ techniques to gain pupils' attention and to stimulate their interest. He may, for example:

1. give them an idea of the relationship between the present lesson and the previous content: and of its relevance to them;

2. introduce the new lesson with some pictures to stimulate their curiosity;

3. review, for a few minutes, the previous day's lesson either by asking pupils to summarize it, or by posing some questions;

4. start the lesson by checking home-work assignments or by analysing the results of a test taken during the preceding day;

5. give them a quiz in vocabulary, spelling or structures, focusing on the items he feels most needed by the pupils;

6. give them a remedial exercise on intonation, rhythm or stress, etc.

After the introductory part which usually occupies five to ten minutes of the lesson time, the teacher moves ahead to the main subject of the lesson to introduce the new material as specified in the Teacher's Book. The teacher is advised not to copy procedures already indicated in the manual. He should write down in his lesson notebook a reference to the procedures or activities described in the Teacher's Book. However, it is preferable for inexperienced teachers to list, with some examples, which words, functions, structures, or communicative abilities, etc. are to be taught. It is also useful to list the activities, strategies or recordings which will be used, without going into details of how and when to use them in the lesson. The amount of material to be taught should fit in the allotted time.

Furthermore, the teacher has to decide, while writing the lesson plan, on the suitable modes or procedures of presentation for different parts of the lesson. Thus he may employ dramatization, role-playing, problem-solving, oral or written reports, discussion, lecturing, grouping, picture-drawing, showing objects, etc. In addition, the teacher has to decide on the teaching aids that are suitable for the lesson and must prepare and examine them before entering the classroom and have them ready at the right time. This is particularly significant if the teacher uses transparencies (overhead-projector) a cassette tape-recorder or filmstrip. To hold the interest of pupils, it is necessary to provide varied activities such as language games and songs. Teachers generally know the types of activities to include in a lesson and how to present them. Success or failure of the lesson largely depends on the teacher's familiarity with the material and on his art of presentation.

This middle part of the lesson usually comprises three phases, namely the teaching point, teacher's activity and pupils' activity. The first phase shows the new material – vocabulary, notions, functions, and structures – to be introduced and practised. The second phase comprises the procedure, the method and the teaching aids to be used by the teacher. The third one includes pupil participation which takes the form of individual, pair or group work activities, spoken or written. It is essential for the teacher, in this part of the lesson presentation, to give opportunities to pupils to express themselves. They should be able to develop the skills of listening, thinking, speaking, and communicating in the foreign language as members of a group. A good lesson plan often contains a number of different activities which provide some practice in the communicative abilities of listening, speaking, reading and writing.

The last stage in lesson planning is the closure in which the teacher re-examines what the pupils have achieved and whether they have understood the day's work. Alternatively, he may review the main points of the lesson.

The teacher must be careful to make the end of the lesson cheerful and interesting, not boring. It must give the pupils the impression that their English language lesson is among the best they experience at school.

Moreover, the teacher must allow a few moments before the end of the lesson to set the assignment for the next day. Homework is an essential ingredient of the learning process. It gives the pupils additional practice in developing their language competence. The forty-five minutes available in the daily school schedule are not sufficient for learning and practising the foreign language, and this shortcoming should be rectified through home-work assignments.

The teacher, therefore, must give the class assignments as frequently as possible. But before giving homework, he should make sure that the assignment is clear to the pupils, is reasonable in length and difficulty, and will help pupils attain the objectives of the lesson. It should also be motivating so that pupils have a feeling of satisfaction in doing it, and it should deal with material already taught or work which pupils can do, bearing directly on the next day's lesson, e.g. finding magazine pictures or making drawings to illustrate a teaching point, or preparing a special project, etc.

With these guidelines in mind, the following types of assignments may be given:

1. Asking the class to find the meanings of a number of new words with the help of a dictionary.

2. Assigning a group of special words or appropriate sentences or a paragraph for spelling practice.

3. Drilling exercises of various types based on the material learnt, or answering comprehension questions on a lesson.

4. Writing a composition, translation or summary-making exercises.

5. Preparing a teaching aid, a bulletin board, a chart or a wall-picture, etc.

6. Assigning two or more pupils to carry out a joint project.

The teacher must check the following day whether each pupil has done the assignment in order to correct it. However, he must not let correction take much time out of a class period. Correction should take no more than five minutes. The teacher or individual pupils may say aloud correct sentences or responses and pupils correct their homework. In addition, the teacher may write the correct answers in advance on an overhead transparency, and uncover the sentences one at a time. Another possible technique is group correction. The teacher divides the class into small groups and each group corrects the homework. The teacher should also explain the difficulties encountered by the pupils, and should reward correct responses.

The teacher should not move abruptly from one teaching point to another. The pace should be normal so that pupils can concentrate and follow the activities at ease. And to avoid boredom, the teacher has to plan lessons in which there is a great deal of variety and pupil participation.

Based on the guidelines discussed above, the following check-list is supplied to help the teacher evaluate the final lesson plan before teaching.[1]

The list is not exhaustive, and teachers can add their own experience to it:

Instructional strategy	Yes	No
— Right for the subject matter	—	—
— Right for the teacher	—	—
— Right for the pupils	—	—
— Right for time available	—	—
— Right for available facilities	—	—
— Right for objectives	—	—

Pupils	Yes	No
— Are the pupils in a position that really allows them to communicate if necessary?	—	—
— Is rearrangement of the classroom necessary to help achieve the aims of the lesson?	—	—
— Does the arrangement of the classroom allow you to have access to the pupils and to move freely?	—	—
— Can the pupils work in comfort?	—	—

Teacher	Yes	No
— Will your personality allow you to successfully carry out the lesson with the above arrangement?	—	—
— Will your position in the classroom allow you to communicate with all the pupils?	—	—
— Can all the pupils see you?	—	—
— Will the instructions and explanations that you give for the stages of the lesson, and the activities be understood by the pupils?	—	—
— Do you have access to all your aids and all the pupils?	—	—

Teaching Aids	Yes	No
— Are they suitable for the lesson?	—	—
— Are they necessary?	—	—
— Do they really help you to fulfil the aims of the lesson?	—	—
— Are they arranged in the room so that you can reach them easily when you need them?	—	—
— Are there any practical reasons why your aids cannot be used?	—	—
— Have you used these aids before?	—	—
— Have you set up the aids properly?	—	—
— Are the aids, especially the mechanical ones, set up and ready when you need them?	—	—
— Are your pupils used to lessons which contain such aids?	—	—
— Have you checked that the material presented on the aids works?	—	—
— Is the information being presented on the aids clear?	—	—

[1] Adapted from Ed Joycey, 'Finalizing the preparation of a lesson', FORUM, Vol. 21/2, 1983.

12.2

Procedures of Lesson Planning

Daily lesson plans need not be lengthy, especially when there is a main course book. However, each lesson plan should include at least the objectives of the particular lesson, an introduction, instructional procedures, application or learning activities, and evaluation. The following steps will illustrate these basic principles:

1. The teacher is advised to review the English syllabus he is going to teach in order to acquaint himself with the material and the goals of the course.

2. He should read the whole unit (i.e. module) before teaching it in order to get a general idea of what is being taught, what topics are to be covered and what the pupils are expected to learn, to accomplish or to do.

3. The teacher should then divide the unit into an appropriate number of teaching steps to ensure that the teaching load is evenly distributed among the various steps.

Concerning the written lesson plan, the teacher should state in a preparation notebook the following guidelines:

(a) The day and date of presentation should be indicated in the margin. Lesson (or number of the step) and page are at the top of the preparation. The teaching point should also be stated briefly.

(b) The aim of the lesson should be stated clearly so that all the activities will be geared towards that aim.

(c) The language points to be taught and materials to be used are made clear.

(d) A brief statement of what the teacher is to do in the first five minutes of the lesson, whether he will check homework, revise previous material – words, functions or structural items, do some remedial work, give a quiz, do a spelling drill, etc.

(e) The teacher is advised to refer to the Teacher's Book for standard teaching procedures that are to be used along with the procedure indicated for each step or lesson.

(f) Pair or group work activities are to be referred to, and so are workbook exercises and cassette recorder drills.

(g) Communicative activities, reading and writing skills or any other application exercises are also to be referred to. Allotted time for this section is between ten and fifteen minutes.

(h) The last five minutes can be devoted to evaluation and assigning homework. The teacher can also ask the class to do a light activity such as a song, a general talk or even tell a joke, so that the pupils may leave the classroom in a good mood. The teacher need not write this down in the lesson plan, unless there is a predetermined homework assignment.

These procedures and the time allotted for each one are not fixed. The classroom situation and the pupils' responses determine the extent and duration of these sections. Moreover, some daily plans require more than one teaching period. At the end, the teacher should write in his preparation notebook a few words on how the lesson was carried out, how much material was not completed or needs further practice, as this will help him in the preparation of the next lesson.

Chapter Thirteen

Classroom Procedures

Introduction

The teacher of English has an important task within the classroom situation. He needs, among other things, a correct theoretical background (i.e. a knowledge of teaching methodology) and considerable skill along with reasonable linguistic competence. Teaching is both a science and an art. The teaching process is more than giving information. It is how to teach, how to design activities and how to involve pupils all the time in these activities. Empirical evidence has shown that pupils cannot communicate in English adequately because they are not given sufficient opportunity to express themselves through speaking and writing.

The most common classroom procedure is for the teacher to ask questions for which he already knows the answers, and for the pupils to listen, repeat and respond without being able to create new utterances. Such a mode of teaching and learning English does not help pupils develop communicative competence neither does it help them in what Rivers calls 'the great leap forward' to communication. The challenge confronting the EFL teacher becomes one of designing techniques and activities which encourage natural communication practice. This is of particular significance in a foreign-language context simply because the classroom constitutes a setting for learning and practising the language. The EFL teacher should, therefore, carry out his task effectively in order to cultivate competence in his pupils. The following procedures will enable the EFL teacher to make his teaching more effective within the limited time allotted for teaching English:

13.1

Prepare Lessons Regularly

It is essential that the teacher prepares for his classes. Prior to starting a lesson the teacher must know the objectives and vocabulary items, language functions, structures, skills, drills and learning activities he plans to conduct. Careful planning saves the teacher's time and effort and enables him to teach effectively.

If an activity does not interest the class, the teacher should abandon it and try another strategy to meet the interests and needs of his pupils.

It is advisable, after the class, for the teacher to ask himself whether he has achieved the objectives and what material he has covered in the teaching period so that he can develop his teaching skills.

13.2
Class Management

Disciplinary problems cause great concern to many teachers. They also lead to frustration. Discipline is essential to a good learning atmosphere and environment. Confusion, on the other hand, hampers instruction and distracts pupils' attention.

The teacher has to arrange the pupils either in rows facing him, or in appropriate groups, or in a semi-circle, depending on the type of activity he is planning to perform. Every pupil in the class should be able to see everyone else. Empty seats should be kept at the back so that pupils are grouped as near the front as possible.

Although firmness is required in the classroom especially with adolescent pupils or when conducting class discussion, the teacher has to create a relaxed atmosphere and to maintain a friendly rapport with students. He must let everyone in the class feel that the teacher cares about their progress and that everyone is called on equally and participates actively in the learning process.

Some pupils are evasive, or afraid to ask or speak for fear of making errors. The teacher's duty is to encourage such pupils to talk in English and to praise their performance and progress, no matter how limited it may be. This encouraging attitude will create a pleasant atmosphere and make English classes lively and enjoyable.

13.3
Speak English in Class

A teacher of English is advised not to speak to his pupils in the mother tongue, or translate from English into Arabic unless absolutely necessary. He has to speak in English as much as possible in class. This is essential in order to improve pupils' hearing and speaking abilities, and to encourage them to communicate in English. However, this requires special care and skill on the part of the teacher to make his use of English in the classroom as efficient as possible. The speed with which he speaks should be suited to the pupils' proficiency in English so that the class can easily understand him and enjoy his teaching. Furthermore, vocabulary, expressions or structures should be carefully chosen so that most of the pupils can understand what he says. However, the teacher must not dominate the situation by talking too much or trying to do the learning work for his pupils. It should always be remembered that it is the pupil who needs to practise speaking, not the teacher, and in order to learn English he must use it. As a general rule, the teacher should not do more than 25 per cent of the talking in the class and the remaining 75 per cent should be done by the pupils so that they get the opportunity to express themselves in English. They, for instance, should know how to discuss different points of view, to express likes and dislikes, to get information and give directions, etc. A good teacher ensures wide participation by asking pupils to formulate questions, conduct communicative activities, prepare instructional material, play games, dramatize conversations and so on.

13.4
Keep the Class Active

An experienced teacher plans the work in a way that keeps the pupils on their toes. The FL teacher must thus provide the class with a wide range of learning activities – for the group and for the individual – which can hold the pupils' attention, and stimulate them to interact and communicate in the language. Such a variety of activities will also prevent boredom and cater for the range of interests of the individuals in the class. Furthermore, since not all pupils are motivated to learn the foreign language, the teacher must devise incentives to arouse interest. He may vary the content, the pace of learning, or the activities of the lesson. In short, the teacher must take account of different levels of aptitude within the class.

13.5
Emphasize Class Discussion

Discussions such as debates, panel talks, mock interviews and the like give a good opportunity to pupils to practise English. This can be done without the kind of control normally imposed by lessons or exercises in grammar, language functions, vocabulary and composition. The teacher must provide opportunities for pupils to express themselves, and to develop skills of listening, thinking, speaking and participating as members of a group. In conducting group activity, the following principles may be taken into consideration:

(a) The teacher should know the abilities and interests of each pupil in the class so that he can organize homogeneous groups.

(b) Maximum pupil participation should be sought. If the discussion is to have general value, each pupil should feel a part of it. However, the teacher should explain the procedure and the problem to be solved.

(c) Pupils should feel that class participation is an important part of the day's lesson.

(d) Every pupil should be given the chance to express his thoughts. The teacher must create an atmosphere in which pupils feel free to state their opinions and to raise questions without constraint.

(e) The teacher should not confine class participation to a few pupils. He should not let individuals dominate the discussion.

(f) Pupils must learn to take turns in talking and to listen while others are speaking. Furthermore, all pupils should be able to hear each other.

(g) The teacher should not correct mistakes in English made during the activity. Correcting errors may discourage or inhibit pupils in their attempts to use the language freely.

(h) The direction of the discussion should be kept under control. Successful activity depends on how well it is presented and on how consciously the teacher controls it. This can be achieved if procedures are established so that discussion allows maximum participation with minimum confusion.

(i) At the end of the activity, the teacher should make final comments, summaries, or give correct responses if required.

13.6
Do Not Over-Correct Pupils' Errors

Correction must be economical. Nothing is less encouraging than constant correction of mistakes when the pupil is concentrating on his ideas. It is desirable to correct serious mistakes and to overlook insignificant ones in order not to complicate the situation.

13.7
Use Appropriate Methods

In devising his strategy, the experienced teacher does not ignore his teaching situation, or the conditions in which his pupils are learning. He takes into consideration psychological and environmental factors that influence the process of foreign language learning and adopts the methods that suit his pupils and meet the objectives of learning. He also varies his techniques and teaching strategies to motivate pupils and facilitate the learning process.

The teacher also clarifies the objectives of the lesson to the pupils to make them aware of what is required. Moreover, he speaks in the classroom in a clear audible voice and writes clearly on the blackboard.

13.8
Encourage External English Practice

Inexperienced teachers and pupils frequently become dependent on the material of the textbook. In such a situation the teacher does not teach, and the pupils do not learn the language adequately simply because they are book-bound. Competent teachers, however, use a textbook as a supplement to their teaching. They are creative in their use of the textbook utilizing its contents in a variety of ways.

The materials of the textbook should, however, act as a stimulus to further study. If pupils have no homework assignments, or do not read books and journals, they will make little progress in the language. The teaching time on the school timetable is insufficient for learning and practising the language. Moreover, external reading consolidates new material and provides pupils with what they need to know. Consequently, the EFL teacher should foster in pupils the habit of further reading and encourage them to practise English outside the classroom.

Chapter Fourteen

Teaching Aids

Introduction

Many aids are utilized for presentation, demonstration, reinforcement and communication practice. The aids can be categorized into four main types, namely: visual, aural, audio-visual and language games. Visual aids include the chalkboard, pictures, posters, drawings, charts, maps, objects, cloth and magnetic boards, plastic figures and cuttings. They also involve projected visuals such as film strips, projectors, overhead projectors and slides. Second, the aural aids comprise radio programmes, taped materials, and the language laboratory. Third, audio-visual aids consist of films, video-tapes, television and microcomputers. Finally, games are of many sorts and levels such as card games, board games and paper and pencil games.

The above mentioned materials and aids are used for (a) stimulating interest in the foreign language; (b) explaining concepts or illustrating meanings; (c) reinforcing learning; (d) directing or promoting conversations in groups; and (e) providing cultural background.

Yet, each type of these aids has its own characteristics and functions. Some of them are more effective than others. Pictures, for example, stimulate more ideas than objects, a chart or overhead projector is more evocative than a chalkboard, newspaper cuttings are easier to handle than real objects, and game-like activities are more useful than others in building communicative competence. Consequently, the teacher should be careful to choose the most appropriate aid that best serves his teaching purposes. The aid should:

(a) be suitable for the teaching objectives;
(b) correlate with the text material or class work;
(c) simplify the learning process;
(d) present or illustrate one point at a time;
(e) draw attention to the purpose it is intended to present;
(f) be of appropriate size and attractive;
(g) provide language experience to improve communicative competence;
(h) evoke interest in the foreign language;
(i) motivate pupils to practise the language individually, in pairs or in groups;

(j) be easy to use or manipulate;

(k) be available in the classroom or school environment.

The teacher and the pupils are advised to establish a classroom library and centre for magazines, newspapers and brochures in the target language, in addition to commercial games, posters, charts, records, coins, stamps, maps and props. The teacher can encourage pupils to provide the centre with a variety of new materials. This chapter will focus on some of the more common aids suitable for use in ELT situations, in order to acquaint the ELT teacher with the effectiveness and limitations of each aid.

14.1

The Blackboard

The blackboard is the most useful and versatile visual aid. It is commonly available in every classroom where it forms a focal point of attention for the whole class. Though a simple aid, the blackboard has several advantages over other aids. One advantage of the blackboard is that anything can be drawn, adjusted, rubbed out and redrawn for a different purpose. Its uses include:

(a) introducing new material;

(b) writing lexical items, new language functions or structural patterns for illustrating their meanings or functions, etc.;

(c) drawing shapes, diagrams or sketches to show relationships or to describe meanings and situations;

(d) writing questions for practice, or model answers for corrections;

(e) training pupils in correct spelling of vocabulary items.

Writing on the blackboard should be clear and neat in order not to confuse pupils. Moreover, the teacher must be careful not to overcrowd the blackboard with too much writing or drawing. It is better to divide the blackboard into three sections each of which can be allotted for a certain task.

14.2

The Cloth/Magnet Board

This aid leads to more active participation in the use of the language. The order of the pictures, cut-outs or cards can be varied to meet the aim of the teaching item. Hence its effectiveness lies in its being a practical device to present, practise, review, dramatize, or enrich language items as well as to motivate verbal response and ensure more effective learning. Thus the teacher may use it in English classes to practise or review personal pronouns, prepositions, basic structural patterns or language functions, and to develop a sequence for telling a story. It can also be used to play games, e.g., a large figure of a human body is cut up, then put together by individual pupils.

14.3

Flash Cards

The main function of flash cards is to teach children English letters and how to start reading. The card is displayed for a few seconds, and then young learners are asked to say what they have just seen either individually, in groups or collectively. This will help them learn to recognize the shape of the letters and to associate each letter or digraph with its most usual sound.

Flash cards can also be used to play games, create dialogues, prepare crossword puzzles and to teach new words or functions. However, the lettering, wording or printing should be neat, clear and large enough to be read by the whole class including those pupils who sit at the back of the class. If flash cards are designed well and displayed adequately they will create competition and stimulation among children who may see them as a change to the class routine worthy of attention.

14.4 Wall Charts

Wall charts are used for introducing new vocabulary, for structure practice, and for straight-forward descriptions. They are particularly valuable for:

(a) practising communication. For example, a chart showing people walking or playing can provide varied utterances, dialogues or conversations,

(b) teaching and revising linguistic forms such as minimal pairs, new vocabulary, prepositions, question words, progressive tense forms, word order, and the like, and

(c) drilling substitutions, as charts with cue words or prompts which are very useful for such drills. The teacher, instead of saying the word, points at the visual prompt on the chart and the pupils place the cue word in the given model sentence or pattern.

Charts should be neat, legible, and large enough to be seen by the whole class. Teachers may encourage pupils to prepare many charts with drawings, or pictures and words. This would motivate them and maintain their interest in the language. Such charts may include tenses of verbs, topics of general interest for class discussion, pictures for composition, diagrams like the vowel triangle and the vocal organs.

14.5 Pictures

EFL teachers find pictures useful:

(a) in teaching, or explaining the meanings of new lexical items or structures;
(b) in practising grammatical points;
(c) in substitution drills;
(d) in stimulating pupils to talk in English;
(e) in developing conversations, dialogues or debates;
(f) in illustrating the content of some reading material;
(g) in teaching short or controlled composition;
(h) in developing pupils' interest in reading;
(i) in developing listening comprehension;
(j) in understanding some aspects of the culture of the people speaking the foreign language.

Teaching pictures are of different types and sizes. There are, for example, slides, colour illustrations, pictures cut from books, journals and magazines and line drawings. In addition, there are picture files for pupils to refer to whenever the occasion arises. However, educational pictures:
(a) should be well selected, simple, clear and interesting;
(b) should be big enough to be seen by everyone in the class;
(c) should not be too detailed although they must show a variety of situations and actions in order to stimulate talking and writing in the foreign language;

(d) should not show objects or experiences which are too familiar to pupils;

(e) should be categorized and arranged according to the subject, e.g. the immediate community, culture of the target language, customs, vocational, leisure-time activities, etc.

It is better to use more than one picture dealing with the same situation and to use them in sequence in order to maintain pupils' motivation and interest.

14.6

The Overhead Projector

Transparencies are used for writing or drawing things to project them onto a screen or a clean wall. This is more effective than the projector which must be used in a darkened classroom. The teacher can easily add and remove the transparencies while teaching. Moreover, he can easily erase the transparencies.

This versatile visual aid has several advantages over the chalkboard. It may be used as an alternative to it for presentation, writing model sentences, question forms, explanation, exercises or for introducing words.

Unlike the blackboard, the teacher need not clean the overhead projector or turn his back on the class when using it. He can keep the class under control and the lesson in progress. Furthermore, the teacher can use the same transparencies several times.

In addition to these advantages, the overhead projector can be used for building up more complex drawings or sentences by placing two or more of the transparencies on top of each other. The teacher may also cut the transparency into smaller pieces to write a word or phrase. This technique is useful in substitution drills or in teaching prepositions, word order or question forms.

The overhead projector can also be used as a large poster. Thus a drawing on a transparency can be projected onto the screen to introduce pictures for demonstration, class discussion or composition writing. The teacher can discuss the items in the poster by pointing to them with a pencil or a long thin stick. Again, this advantage of the overhead projector helps the teacher direct the discussion or activity while projection is in progress without losing control of the class.

14.7

Slides and Filmstrips

These two visual aids are not commonly used in English classes although they provide a convenient and relatively economical means of presenting information to different classes.

14.8

The Tape-recorder

The tape-recorder as a classroom aid forms an integral part of English instruction. It is an effective means of developing the pupils' communicative competence. Thus the tape:

(a) can be used to motivate interest in the foreign language as pupils respond enthusiastically when they hear voices speaking English with native fluency and accent; or when they listen to their own recorded voices.

(b) can provide a good opportunity to hear voices other than their teacher's and voices of native speakers of English. This advantage gives the pupils valuable practice in listening to and imitating the pronunciation and intonation of natural standard English. For such a drill, pupils who have cassette recorders can tape radio broadcasts or plays and talks and bring them into the classroom as accurate models of English.

(c) can supplement or reinforce learning by providing correct and consistent models of poetry, dialogues and plays for pupils to imitate.

(d) can add realism and interest to English classes by introducing the outside world (conversations in shops, playgrounds, etc.) into the classroom.

(e) can help pupils develop their aural comprehension skill. They may listen to recorded speech and identify objects in a picture as they are mentioned on the tape.

However, for effective use of the tape recorder and recordings, the following points should be considered:

(a) The teacher and pupils should get tape/cassette recorders of good tone quality.

(b) They should know how to operate the machine.

(c) The recordings should be clear, comprehensible and at a normal speed so as to enable pupils to understand the taped material and respond accordingly.

(d) The pauses betweeen items (e.g. questions and answers, drills, instructions, directions, etc.) should be adequate for correct or appropriate responses.

14.9

The Language Laboratory

The language laboratory as a teaching aid is not used on a large scale in our schools. It is too expensive to buy and run effectively, and partly because the time allotted for teaching the foreign language, i.e. English, is limited. However, as a supplementary facility, the language laboratory is mainly used for individual intensive practice of what has been learnt. The advantages of the language laboratory can be summed up as follows:

(a) It is an effective means of practising listening comprehension.
(b) It is a useful aid for enhancing the teaching of short sentences.
(c) It is an effective tool for pronunciation drills – stress, rhythm and intonation, and for communication practice.
(d) It is a useful device for consolidating structures and language functions.
(e) It is also useful for testing aural/oral language skills – listening, speaking or reading.
(f) It allows pupils to work at their own speed and to correct themselves.
(g) It gives pupils more time for speaking in the foreign language than they would have in the conventional classroom.
(h) It stimulates shy pupils to practise in the language as it gives them a sense of privacy, when listening and repeating, etc.
(i) It helps the teacher cope with the individual differences which could not possibly be dealt with properly in the classroom.

(j) It allows the teacher to listen or speak to the pupils individually or together.

(k) It also provides a stimulus for such activities as note-taking, report writing, written and oral answers based on the listening comprehension.

However, the language lab. does not necessarily secure fluency to every pupil because much of its material is in the form of structural drills based on stimulus–response and correct answer.

The teacher is advised (a) not to use the lab. for new presentation so as to avoid wasting the recording facilities; (b) to prepare the class for the kind of work they will be practising in the lab.; (c) to follow this with work in the classroom to reinforce the experiences the pupils have in the lab., and (d) to choose appropriate material including a variety of activities to make language laboratory work motivating.

14.10

Other Aids

In addition to the previously mentioned aids, there are other electrical aids which may vitalize teaching and motivate pupils. However, these aids are not commonly used in schools because the teachers may not be inclined to make use of them. Some of these aids will be discussed briefly.

The radio has pedagogic value as it provides models of good native speech for pupils to improve their pronunciation, oral fluency and aural comprehension. It is advisable to encourage pupils to tape English programmes broadcast on the radio and to bring them into the class for discussion.

Television is a teaching aid which makes learning experiences concrete and realistic. It also plays an effective role in developing linguistic and communicative skills. The EFL teacher should encourage pupils to watch newscasts and dramas, if an English-speaking channel or English programmes are available.

Videotapes are useful for specialized study and for filming trainee teachers, or the pupils as they act out dialogues and other language activities. The teacher can stop the video when he wants to check the recordings, go forward or backward for correction.

Films are pleasant and rewarding teaching aids. They provide situations which can be used for teaching composition, comparing experiences and language practice. The teacher, however, should choose the films carefully, preview them to check their educational value and prepare drills about events, characters, descriptions, etc., for oral practice.

The computer as an instructional aid, is gaining widespread acceptance. Computer applications in foreign language learning have not, as yet, been introduced into Arab schools. However, it is expected that computers will be used in the near future owing to their great usefulness in demonstration, drill and practice.

14.11

Games

Some commercial games lend themselves to foreign language learning as instructional aids and as a pleasant change of classroom procedure. They can be useful, especially in the intermediate school, since young learners enjoy playing games and respond positively to them. The EFL teacher should ensure that the activity contributes to furthering the linguistic and communicative aims of the foreign language syllabus. The game, for example, should:

(a) involve more than one player in order to stimulate the pupils to interact and communicate in the foreign language;
(b) retain the interest of all pupils to avoid boredom;
(c) be simple to manipulate;
(d) be brisk so that young learners will not become bored;
(e) have a learning objective and not just be a game for fun. That is, games should be selected primarily for their educational value and not merely as moments of relaxation.

Chapter Fifteen

The Importance
of Motivation

Motivation is a basic element in foreign language teaching and learning. Empirical studies indicate that highly motivated pupils learn faster and better than the ones who find the study of language distasteful. Hence the need for pedagogical motivation. This refers to the ability to arouse in the pupils a desire to learn the language and a feeling that the language they are learning is useful. Failure to do this will impose a severe limitation on the learning process. Ideally, motivation should come from the learners or be based primarily on their desires and needs. But this is not easy to achieve with school-children between the ages of ten and eighteen. They are still not mature enough to understand the goals or objectives underlying foreign language learning. Their interest is not strong, especially at the intermediate stage, when they make the first contact with English.

In addition, the teacher may not be familiar with the needs of his pupils. Even if he is, how can he cater for individual interests in large mixed classes?

Unfortunately, the ideal teaching and learning situation may exist only in private institutions where the foreign language is usually taught for special purposes. Motivation in such settings does not present any problem to the teacher, because the pupils are internally motivated to learn the foreign language. The situation is different with the Arab state schools where classes have on average thirty pupils each and pupils range from the highly motivated to the poorly motivated. If the teacher wanted to discover the various motives of each pupil, the whole process would be time-consuming.

It often happens that there is only one foreign language, namely English, on the timetable of Arab schools. All pupils in the Arab countries must learn it and have no choice in this. The issue of motivation is thus transformed into creating the desire among them to learn the foreign language. How to meet this issue is the function of external motivation without which the pupils' interest in the language will gradually decline. In other words, if the teachers do not provide incentives to induce children to learn the language, their achievement will inevitably be meagre. Everything depends on the teacher, the materials, including audio-visual aids, the quality of teaching and classroom activities. As the language is taught in a foreign context with little reinforcement from the immediate environment, success or failure in learning the language largely depends on such incentives as good quality teaching, appropriate texts and aids, communicative activities and the learning setting. Such incentives form the driving force that makes the process of teaching more effective. The teacher himself represents a strong motivational factor. Thus his interest, competence and perseverance determine the degree of success of any language course.

It is clear, from the foregoing, that primary motivation in which the interest comes from the learner is an ideal situation not often met, and that secondary motivation in which the interest comes from outside the learner is more important in school pupils. In other words, it is the teaching process that has the greatest influence on the learner's motivation. Such motivation is under the control of the teacher who directs the learning process to sustain the pupils' interest in learning the language.

The teacher, first of all, has to give the pupils clear and detailed information about the aims of their learning and to relate the aims to their needs. Moreover, he must explain to them how this knowledge of the foreign language will be useful for them in their future careers. For this purpose he must set down both short- and long-term objectives for their learning; objectives which must be under constant review to maintain relevance.

The teacher must show genuine interest in his pupils and their achievements. Nothing is more disappointing for a pupil than to feel ignored, neglected, or carelessly evaluated, or to feel that his work does not appeal to the teacher. An encouraging attitude on the part of the teacher motivates pupils and makes them interested in learning the language.

In order to increase pupils' participation, the teacher must employ techniques that require the pupils to utilize the language creatively as an instrument of learning. In this regard, he can provide them with effective communication skills and with an understanding of the foreign language culture.

A variety of classroom activities play an essential part in motivating students and facilitating the acquisition of a foreign language. They can reduce the strain of formality in the classroom and make learning more pupil-centred and less teacher-centred. Activities carried out in groups where students exchange personally relevant information may help to motivate and encourage the more diffident pupils. Activities transfer the process of learning from 'skill-getting' to 'skill-using'. Activities that can motivate the pupils include role-playing, problem-solving, mock interviews, classroom debates, contests in writing stories and learning and presenting playlets. The learning situation and the teacher's imagination can suggest many other activities which can be stimulating to the pupils.

However, motivation in language learning is situation-specific; that is to say what applies to one situation or community may not apply to another. For example, a learner of English in Germany is motivated differently from one in the Arab world. The former could appreciate the need for conversational English to help him seek essential information when visiting an English-speaking country. On the other hand, a pupil from the Arab world may foresee the need for skills in reading and writing English to help him find a job or when pursuing his university studies.

same community, motivation variables may vary according to geographical differences. Thus metropolitan students, who are usually exposed to many varieties of English usage are more motivated than rural children. Connected with this is the socio-economic factor which has some influence on the pupils' achievement. Children of educated parents can achieve high levels of performance in the foreign language and vice versa. This state of affairs actually reflects the complexity of motivating variables which do not occur singly, but co-exist and interact.

In conclusion, teachers cannot depend completely on the pupils' interests and desires for learning a foreign language. Consequently, external motives are the most important elements in successful foreign language learning and are adequate compensatory factors for the absence of the spontaneous desire to learn the language.

Chapter Sixteen

Language Testing

Introduction

This chapter will focus on the current system of evaluation in our schools. It also examines its validity and effectiveness in the light of communicative methodology.

In addition some suggestions will be made for improving the process of testing. The chapter concludes with a glossary of testing terms. It may be added that there are several sources that deal with the procedures and assumptions of foreign language testing (see Andrew 1980, Harris 1969, Lado 1961, Oller 1979, Vallette 1969).

16.1

Testing in Schools

Testing plays a crucial role in teaching and learning English. It enables teachers and pupils to evaluate the achievement of their goals. Teachers can track the progress of their pupils. That is, how well they are mastering the content so that teachers can determine or modify their plans to meet the problems faced by students. On the other hand, pupils benefit from tests as they stimulate them to pay closer attention to the material. They also give them feedback about the strong and weak areas in their performance, so that they can remedy their weaknesses.

In addition, tests are allotted a pre-eminent position in Arab World school systems. Thus apart from their main function as a tool for measuring achievement, promotion and graduation, they also serve as a basis for reporting pupils' progress to the people concerned. Empirical evidence has shown that motivation to study English is related to examination. Pupils endeavour to score high grades in order to be able to join higher institutes where admission is based on mark aggregation.

A pupil who has an average score of more than 90 per cent, for instance, is eligible for admission to medical school, while a pupil with a slightly lower average, would join the engineering faculty. Such a system undoubtedly has an adverse effect on pupils' achievement since it confines their motivation to the attainment of high marks. However, in the following sections, some issues in our system of pupil assessment will be reviewed.

16.2

Pupil Evaluation Systems

Schools in the Arab world depend almost exclusively on achievement tests. These are school tests, classroom tests, written tests, oral tests, home tests, and integrative tests.[1] They are aspects of teacher-made tests constructed mainly to assess the pupils' ability to use the foreign language in terms of marks. These marks are used to assess the pupil's level of achievement and the progress he has made.

Such a system of evaluation is difficult to justify from a practical point of view because it does not tell us what a pupil actually knows, and what level of communicative competence he has attained. The pupil's work is judged by the total mark he gets although he may be poor in the language. Pupils often score a high mark in one of the language skills or elements such as reading, translation or vocabulary. However, this mark overlooks the fact that he may be deficient in other areas of the language. Thus emphasis on the mark rather than on learning is a drawback in our system of evaluation.

16.3

Objectives and Testing

Because the method of measuring pupils' achievement is restricted to 'paper and pencil' tests, aural/oral skills can find no place in the current testing process. This is a clear indication that it is inadequate. That is, it does not cater for aural/oral fluency, an objective emphasized strongly by both the audio-lingual and the communicative approaches. It is paradoxical that while the aural/oral skills are emphasized by the structural and the notional–functional syllabuses, they are eliminated completely from the promotional or terminal examinations. Even in monthly tests, they are treated superficially as they are assessed according to the impressions of the teacher. The absence of the oral component in the process of testing affects motivation adversely. It hinders the development of aural/oral skills and eventually reduces the pupils' interest in foreign language learning.

16.4

Test Construction

Our promotional tests are normally prepared by one or two teachers of the English staff. The tests sometimes result from casual meetings of language teachers who choose materials for the examinations subjectively. Writing a blueprint for the test or running an item analysis is not considered when preparing the test. Most of the test items are usually copied from the textbook. Furthermore the test items are not necessarily graded with respect to difficulty. The first and the last item of each section are nearly of the same level of difficulty. Although the test is relatively long and contains objective and subjective items, the degree of variation is too narrow to allow discrimination between levels of achievement.

Individual differences are also overlooked in the sense that the same test is taken by all pupils of the same grade of form regardless of their abilities or progress through the course. Although all pupils study the same syllabus, some of them cannot assimilate or cover the text material. Consequently, it is unfair to give the same test items to all pupils. In order to overcome this problem the items need to range from those that nearly everyone can answer to others that only able pupils can tackle. Otherwise it is difficult to achieve tests that are valid, reliable and discriminating.

[1] See glossary at the end of this chapter.

16.5
Monthly Tests

The system of monthly or half-quarterly tests has a restrictive effect upon the process of teaching and learning. They are time-consuming and require effort in preparing, conducting and marking. Series of monthly tests along with continued assessment cause stress and disturbance to the teachers and pupils alike.

In the first place, tests put the teacher under a heavy responsibility to force pupils through the allotted monthly examination work in a given time. In addition, frequent testing makes the teachers reluctant to introduce learning experiences or practise satisfactorily. Teachers are also restricted by these tests because they minimize their contact with individual pupils and prevent them from helping the less able ones.

The pupils are also dissatisfied with these frequent tests. Tests force upon them a constant anxiety to succeed rather than to take pleasure in the educational experience. Furthermore tests adversely affect pupils' interest and motivation in learning the foreign language as they often have to struggle with the tests. This state of affairs prevents pupils, especially the less able ones, from having time to learn and practise the target language effectively.

It is thus advisable to reduce the frequency of testing to four tests, including mid-term and final examinations, throughout the school year. Continuing assessment should also be modified. It must consist of short quizzes to occupy a small part of the teaching period. The teacher should assign the test material, fix a certain date in advance or give quizzes at regular intervals, so as not to disturb pupils.

16.6
On-going Assessment

Testing should be an integral part of instruction. The main purpose is to know how well the pupils have mastered each step or unit so that teachers can make necessary modifications in the process of teaching. For these reasons assessment should be present in almost every lesson.

Nevertheless experience indicates that this process of evaluation has been misused by the majority of EFL teachers. They erroneously substitute for it monthly or regular tests. It may be pointed out that continued assessment, need not be based on paper and pencil tests. They may be oral or written questions, reports and summaries. These tests may also include silent observation of pupils at work, or calling for a summary of the given lesson or material. The advantage of such evaluation techniques is that teachers do not devote so much time and effort to constructing written paper and pencil tests.

16.7
Testing Communicative Competence

Many institutions of foreign language teaching in the Arab world have adopted a communicatively designed syllabus with its emphasis on purposive and interactive language use. Even those institutions which are still employing a structurally-oriented syllabus are stressing oral skills as essential components of foreign language learning. Such important objectives should therefore be reflected in testing tasks in order to make achievement tests valid and meaningful. But this is not the case with the testing methods which are currently used. They tend to stress the discrete features of language, and not the overall language proficiency or communicative competence of the pupils. That is, the focus is on testing the linguistic forms – vocabulary, grammar, pronunciation, spelling, composition, reading comprehension, translation, etc. A major shortcoming of this process is that it is not completely integrative; it excludes listening comprehension and speaking from its components. Moreover, the items designed to test communicative competence are not varied.

Communicative competence, however, can be tested both on the receptive and on the productive level. The former may include, for example, recognition of formal or informal language, appropriate and tactful response, matching utterances, reactions or communicative expressions, and the like. Productive knowledge can be judged through oral or written activities such as making comments, reactions to statements showing disagreement or engaging in role-playing, completing dialogues, conducting an interview, etc.

As for testing communicative abilities, namely, aural comprehension, speaking, reading and writing, the following procedures are recommended.[1] (See Part 4 for suggested activities for developing communicative abilities.)

Listening Comprehension

1. Listen and point: the teacher shows the class various pictures. He then describes one of the pictures, asking the pupils to distinguish it from the others.

2. Listen and recognize: pupils listen to an appropriate text. They then state the meaning of certain vocabulary items, the form of items whether singular or plural, count or non-count, etc., or tenses of verbs, whether present, past or future, etc.

3. Listen and write: the teacher presents the class with a dialogue, a story or a conversation. Pupils listen one or more times and then answer questions about the content. It is preferable to write the questions on the chalkboard before the pupils listen to the test. This gives them some idea of the information they are looking for. The teacher is also advised to avoid questions which require details.

   As a variation of this technique, pupils listen to radio broadcasts, or to television shows. Pupils can be tested directly by using the appropriate media and the same method as above.

4. Listen and answer: the teacher gives oral messages, or conveys some information or instructions, etc. The pupils answer questions by means of which the teacher determines how much they have understood. Again, it is preferable to give the class the questions beforehand. The questions can be of a true–false type as the information required is specific and direct.

5. Participate and be tested: the pupils may participate in an oral activity (e.g. an interview, a role-play or a conversation). The pupils then can be tested directly during the activity. The teacher observes the quality of interaction through gestures, questions, comments, and the like.

Speaking

Evaluating speaking ability is a difficult task as it takes more time to administer to a large class than commonly-used discrete point linguistic tests. This reason (i.e. lack of time) may explain why teachers avoid examinations of oral fluency and the ability to communicate ideas appropriately. Thus the ability to speak is tested through an overall impression in most cases. This way seems more practical as the teacher need not designate a special day or time for oral fluency exams. By observing pupils' interaction and participation in class activities he can judge their oral ability. However, the following testing techniques might be of some help in this regard.

1. Pupils participate in a dialogue, a debate, a classroom conversation, etc.

2. Pupils narrate, tell jokes, recount events, give instructions, talk about familiar topics, etc., for a limited duration of time.

3. Pupils engage in formal talks or speeches such as class reports, panels, arguments, etc.

4. Pupils may be asked questions of general interest to which they answer in two or more sentences.

5. Pupils may be asked to describe orally a picture, a situation, an event, etc.

6. Pupils may be interviewed by the teacher who asks open-ended questions about topics and situations the pupils have been dealing with.

Reading Ability

Reading skills are varied – skimming, scanning, silent, oral, pleasure reading. Each has its own testing technique. Thus for oral reading, individual pupils read an unfamiliar passage aloud, then they answer questions on the content, or characters in the passage, or give definitions of selected words or functions, etc. By contrast, in reading for comprehension, pupils read the assigned passage within a limited time, and subsequently answer a variety of questions such as objective type items, vocabulary completion with reference to the text, making a summary or indicating allusions to and facts about the target culture, etc.

Instead of reading passages, the teacher may provide the class with selected forms, signs or advertisements written in English and then ask questions which test the pupils' comprehension.

For scanning and skimming tests, the teacher provides the class with excerpts from English newspapers. The pupils read the material silently and work out a problem or write the main point of the text. However, for pleasure or free reading, the pupils read appropriate stories, then answer questions which test comprehension.

Writing Ability

There are many techniques to test writing skills. Some of the important procedures are:

1. inserting punctuation marks, capital letters;
2. writing full words for numerals, symbols or abbreviations;
3. constructing sentences from scrambled words;
4. putting dialogue sentences in correct order;
5. answering questions on a dialogue;
6. filling in crossword puzzles;
7. filling out forms;
8. matching questions and answers;

9. writing from dictation;
10. completing sentences or dialogue from cues;
11. expanding basic sentence patterns by adding logical details;
12. answering questions by using maps, overhead transparencies, magazine articles;
13. translating from the language into the target language;
14. changing a narrative to a dialogue;
15. retelling a story from another person's point of view;
16. rewriting a passage to change the tenses of verbs;
17. writing guided composition from specific instructions, or given expressions and vocabulary;
18. writing a résumé of a passage recorded on tape;
19. formulating questions on a passage;
20. writing personal or business letters;
21. creating situations with the help of verbal cues, props, visual cues;
22. completing or expanding a story;
23. writing essays, fiction or poetry;
24. taking a cloze test, etc.

16.8
Characteristics of a Good Test

A good test should possess the following qualities:

(a) Validity. A valid test measures what it ought to be testing. For example, a test that is designed to measure control of grammar becomes invalid if it contains difficult vocabulary.

(b) Reliability. A test should provide consistency in measuring the items being evaluated. In other words, if the same test is given twice to the same pupils, it should produce almost the same results.

(c) Practicality. A practical test is easy to administer and to score without wasting too much time or effort.

(d) Comprehension. A good test should be comprehensive, covering all the items which have been studied. This enables teachers to know accurately the extent of the pupils' knowledge.

(e) Relevance. The items of an effective test should measure reasonably well the desired objectives or achievement.

(f) Balance. A practical test evaluates both linguistic and communicative competence. That is, the items of the test must reflect the pupils' real command of the language with regard to appropriateness and accuracy.

(g) Economy. An efficient test makes best use of the teacher's limited time for preparing and grading, and of the pupils' assigned time for answering all the items. Thus oral exams with classes of thirty or more pupils are not economical since they require too much time and effort.

(h) Authenticity. The language of a test should reflect everyday discourse.

(i) Difficulty. The test questions should be appropriate in difficulty, neither too hard nor too easy. Moreover, the questions should be progressive in difficulty in order to reduce stress and tension.

(j) Clarity. It is essential that all questions and instructions should be clear so as to enable pupils to know exactly what the examiner wants them to do.

(k) Objectivity. The questions and answers should be clear and definite so that the marker would give the score a pupil deserves.

(l) Time. A good test is one that is appropriate in length for the allotted time.

16.9

Glossary of Terms (see Cohen (1980) for further terms)

Achievement test: Used to discover how much has been learned.

Cloze procedure: A test construction procedure that involves deleting words on a systematic basis and replacing the deletions with blanks which the pupil must fill in.

Criterion-referenced test: Used to determine how many pupils have attained a given level of proficiency. Their performances are compared with the attainment of the objectives of instruction.

Diagnostic test: Aims to discover particular points of difficulty pupils may encounter.

Discrete-point test: Evaluated control of specific linguistic items.

Distractor: An alternative-response choice which is intended to attract pupils who do not know the right answer.

General proficiency test: Measures total competence in the foreign language. It includes a wide range of skills and elements such as listening comprehension, reading comprehension, writing ability, grammar, vocabulary, pronunciation, etc.

Integrative test: Used for assessing more than one item, e.g. to evaluate listening comprehension and speaking or writing.

Item analysis: Looking at the results of a test in terms of item difficulty and item discrimination.

Language aptitude test: Designed to discover whether pupils possess a talent or a basic ability for learning a new language. It includes exercises in number learning, phonetic script, spelling clues, function of words in sentences, and memorization of paired associate words.

Linguistic competence: The breadth of knowledge that the learner has regarding the elements of the language – pronunciation, vocabulary and structure.

Mean score: The average score for a given group of pupils obtained by adding all the individual scores and then dividing by the total number of pupils.

Minimal pair: Two words sounding alike in all but one feature, e.g. 'heating', 'hitting'.

Native language: The first language acquired as a mother tongue.

Norm-referenced test: Used to rank pupils. The teacher compares individual pupils' performances against the achievement of other pupils who were subjected to the same test.

Proficiency test: A measure of the linguistic knowledge that pupils have and/or their ability to apply this knowledge functionally.

Quiz: A short test of class material, generally informal in nature.

Raw score: The score obtained directly as a result of totalling all the items answered correctly on a test.

Reliability: The degree to which a test produces similar results on different occasions under similar conditions.

Scoring a test: Determining the number of points that each item or procedure is to receive, and then the value or weighting of these points with respect to the total test or quiz.

Standardized test: A carefully designed test that has undergone long experimentation and research. It is often administered to large groups of pupils from different types of schools.

Test point: Any feature or form that a given item elicits. It includes both points intended to be tested by the item and all the points actually elicited by a given item.

Test item: One entry or question on a test or quiz.

Validity: The degree to which a test actually measures what it is supposed to measure.

Appendix I:
Components of
Communicative Competence

1.
Linguistic Competence

Linguistic competence constitutes the core of the communication act, i.e. receiving and giving messages, meanings or functions. It is impossible to imagine a person being communicatively competent without being linguistically competent. This competence encompasses the following elements:

(a) phonology pronunciation including segmental phonemes and suprasegmental features;

(b) orthographic rules – spelling of words;

(c) grammar (in its broad sense);

(d) lexis – words/vocabulary of the language.

2.
Pragmatic Competence

This provides the link between linguistic competence and actual language use in specific situations. It contains the following elements:

Language functions

(a) *expressive utterances:* These involve the speaker's attitude, opinion, feeling, interjection, etc.

(b) *directive utterances:* They focus on the addressee, for example, when someone is being asked or told to do something.

(c) *referential function:* This focuses on that setting, or that part of the context which is being talked about or referred to.

(d) *phatic function:* This focuses on contact between participants. It serves to establish, maintain or discontinue communication. Examples: hello, how are you, bye, see you, etc.

(e) *metalinguistic:* When the focus is on the code, the function of the utterance is metalinguistic. The function also refers to explanations and comments about speech acts, e.g.: I repeat, I must emphasize, what does this word mean? I don't understand, etc.

(f) *poetic function:* This covers all uses of language in which message form is of primary importance, for example children's rhymes, alliteration in advertising, aesthetic effects in poetry, etc.

Speech Acts

These are divided into three major types of acts: attitudinal, informative, and ritual.

(a) *Attitudinal acts:* These refer to:
   (i) past events – apologize, justify, excuse, reject, disagree, agree, complain, forgive, congratulate, etc.
   (ii) future events, e.g. intend, offer, promise, request, suggest, permit, etc.

(b) *Informative acts:* These state factual information, express opinions, express emotional attitudes, explain, report, recommend, regret, etc.

(c) *Ritual acts:* These are classified on the basis of how they relate to the opening and closing of a communicative event – greeting and taking leave.

Discourse Strategy

This refers to a structured text that constitutes sequences of speech acts rather than a jumble of unrelated utterances. This strategy involves the following aspects:

(a) *Coherence:* This is a way in which structure is created in texts as in the sequential characteristic of speech acts. Discourse is established in texts when a speech act conditions another speech act or when it is conditioned by previous speech acts, as in adjacency pairs like the question/answer pair or initiating/responding acts. It is also established through ties between the content or propositions expressed by different acts.

(b) *Cohesion:* This is the creation of ties between sentences, by lexical and grammatical means, e.g. anaphoric references, elliptical constructions, conjunctions, adverbials and adverbial phrases such as: and, but, however, on the other hand, etc.

(c) *Gambits:* These are words and expressions that help regulate conversation, e.g. well, now, oh yes, but, awfully nice, aha, mm, yeah, er, etc.

(d) *Turn-taking:* In conversations and dialogues this refers to the change from one speaker to another. Turn-taking is made possible by a verbal or non-verbal bid, e.g. so that's what we're going to do, that was all I wanted to know, that's fine . . . , I'm afraid I have to dash now, etc., or by completing an initiating act, or by gazing or looking at the listener.

(e) *Repair work:* This means that either the speaker or the listener 'repairs' something the speaker has said and which appears to be a problem. Examples: He wants to study philosophy – not philosophy (self-initiated-repair). He wants to study psychology. The listener initiates a repair: psychology you mean! (other-initiated, interactional repair).

   This technique of 'repair work' is used to clarify the communication of an idea that was formulated incorrectly.

3. Strategic Competence

This is the speaker's ability to solve communication problems by means of strategies. The term covers problem-solving devices that learners resort to in order to solve what they experience as problems in speech production and reception. It involves two aspects, namely: strategies in production and strategies in reception.

Strategies in production: When the EFL learner cannot find the word or expression needed, the choices open to him are:

(a) to give up completely, or
(b) to reduce his communicative intention, or
(c) to make use of his mother tongue, or
(d) to paraphrase, using other English words, or
(e) to construct a new interlanguage word, or

(f) to appeal for help from participants, or

(g) to use gestures and facial expressions as in direct contact with the addressee.

Strategies in reception: When an EFL learner is unable to comprehend or infer meaning, he may resort to an interactional strategy. That is, he would request the interlocutor to self-repair, simply by saying 'I don't understand', or 'I don't know, or what do you mean?' etc.

4.
Socio-Cultural Competence

Elements of communicative competence cannot be separated from social competence. The EFL learners' communicative competence will remain inadequate unless they know the appropriate context for their use. Ignorance of cultural features would either create misunderstanding or lead to incapacity to use the language.

The social use of the language involves, among other things, cultural allusions or conventions such as ways of thinking, customs, mores, art forms, idioms, beliefs, etc.

Pragmatic as well as speech act knowledge is a clear instance of communicative competence interacting with social competence.

5.
Fluency Competence

This refers to the ability to express oneself quickly and easily. In other words it is the capacity to be able to put what one wants to say into words with ease. However, fluency is not synonymous with fast speech or correctness. One can be fluent and incorrect, fluent and correct but unable to talk fast, or not fluent and correct.

There are three different types of fluency:

Semantic Fluency: Linking together propositions and speech acts. That is coherence.

Lexical-Syntactic Fluency: Linking together syntactic constituents and words.

Articulatory Fluency: Linking together speech segments.

Symptoms of non-fluent speech are pauses, false starts, self-corrections, repetitions, not knowing what to say or how to say something, difficulty in pronouncing particular sounds (e.g. stuttering), lack of confidence, frequent filled pauses (er, erm, I mean, you know), etc.

To round off this discussion, reference may be made to the notion of metacommunicative awareness as a teaching objective within EFL instruction. This concept means conscious knowledge about the components of communicative competence, their interdependence and social function. It is inefficient learning to know about the vocabulary of the language and its rules of grammar and pronunciation unless they are related to pragmatic and social considerations. This means that metalinguistic knowledge (i.e. knowledge about grammar, phonology and lexis) should have a sense of cultural relativism so that pupils will become proficient in communication.

Appendix II:
Glossary of
Language Functions

1. Asking for information:
I wonder if you could help me . . .
I'd like to know . . .
I wonder if you could tell me . . .
I hope you don't mind my asking, but I'd like to know . . .
Could you please tell . . .?
Can I have . . . please?
Would you mind . . .ing . . .?
Do you think you could . . . please?
Would you be so kind as to . . .
Do you happen to know . . .?

2. Asking for further information:
Could you please explain this more clearly?
Could you tell me a bit more?
What I'd like to know is . . .
What do you mean exactly?
And what else do you know?
I would be grateful for some further information.
Something else I'd like to know is . . .
Sorry to press you, but could you tell me . . .
Sorry, I don't quite understand why . . .

3. Suggestions:
I suggest . . .
How about . . .
Why don't we . . .
He could . . .
Couldn't we . . .
Why not . . .

What about . . .
There's always . . .
Let's . . .
If you ask me . . .
Have you . . .
Why don't you try . . .
It would be a good idea . . .
I think you should . . .
We might . . .
I was wondering if you'd ever thought of . . .
Might be an idea to . . .

4. Expressing pleasure and liking:
This is just what I need . . .
I am very glad you've . . .
What a pleasure!
I'm pleased to meet you.
It will give me much pleasure to . . .
This is very nice (pleasant).
I can't tell you how happy I am . . .
I'm really pleased . . .
How marvellous . . .
It gives me great pleasure to . . .
I enjoy (visiting) . . .

5. Expressing dislike and displeasure:
How unpleasant! How awful! What a shame . . .
I dislike . . .
What are the disadvantages . . .
Must you behave in this unpleasant way!

He is rather offended.
He is quite displeased.
I don't enjoy his company.
This is not very nice/pleasant.
I'm not pleased . . .
It will give me much trouble to . . .

6. Inquiring about pleasure/displeasure:
Do you like/enjoy . . . ?
Don't you like/enjoy . . . ?
Would you . . .
Is it all right now?
Is this what you want?

7. Expressing satisfaction:
This is very good/nice . . .
It is quite all right now . . .
This is just what I want/need/mean . . .
This is just what I had in mind . . .
I'm satisfied . . .
I'm really satisfied . . .
It gives me great pleasure . . .
He is content with . . .
We were all gratified with . . ./at the result.
It gratified me to know . . .
I have enjoyed . . .

8. Expressing dissatisfaction:
I don't like this . . .
This is not right yet.
This is not what I need/want . . .

9. Enquiring about (dis)satisfaction:
Do you like this?
Is it all right now?
Is this what you need?

10. Expressing fear or worry:
I'm afraid . . .
I'm worried . . .
You aren't afraid, are you?
Are you afraid/worried?

11. Expressing surprise:
This is a surprise . . .
What a surprise . . .
It's surprising . . .
It's rather amazing/astonishing . . .
Wasn't it extraordinary that . . . ?
Surprisingly/strangely/incredibly . . .

12. Expressing approval:
Good! Excellent! Splendid! Marvellous! Fantastic!
    Wonderful!
Terrific! Magnificent! Fascinating!

I (very much) approve of the plan.
It wasn't bad . . . , was it?
I like . . . I do like . . . I rather like . . .
What a great . . .
You're extremely good.
Did you really do that . . . ?
You're extremely good.
I approve of that . . .

13. Expressing disapproval:
You shouldn't listen to . . .
You shouldn't have done that . . .
It's not very nice . . .
I'm all against it . . .
I'd rather you didn't . . .
How awful . . . How unpleasant . . .
I didn't enjoy . . .
Just look at it . . .
That's ridiculous/stupid . . .
She should think of something more sensible.
I disapprove of . . .
Bad . . . Too much . . . Too little . . . None . . .
Oh dear! That won't do!
You're no good.
That's not the right way to . . .
You'll have to do better than that . . .
You are to blame . . .
I take a poor view of . . .
Do you think this is all right.
That's a great pity.

14. Expressing apologies and excuses:
Oh dear, I'm awfully sorry.
I am terribly sorry.
I do apologize. Excuse me for . . .
I'm sorry I/that . . .
It's not my fault . . .
I can't tell you how sorry I am.
I'm so sorry, I didn't realize.
Please forgive me.
Don't blame me.
Don't worry.
How can I make it up to you . . .
If only I . . .

15. Expressing indifference:
I am not interested in . . .
It doesn't matter . . .
I don't mind . . .
I don't mind if you don't come . . .
I don't care . . .

16. Expressing interest:
That's very interesting.
I'm interested in . . .

17. Expressing opinion:

In my opinion . . .
I think . . . a good idea/a bad idea.
They are marvellous.
They are ridiculous.
As I see it . . .
As for me . . .
My point of view is . . .
I believe that . . .
Let's say . . .
It's my belief . . .
I agree that . . .
On the other hand . . .
My first point was . . .
Surely . . .
It's a matter of taste . . .
You must agree.
Honestly . . .
If you ask me . . .
Well, it is only my opinion, but . . .

18. Expressing agreement:

Sure, I'll be glad to . . .
I agree . . .; by all means . . .
That's right . . .
Of course . . . Exactly . . . correct . . .
Why not? Why, yes of course.
I am with you.
Agreed.
It is just that.
I'm with the idea . . .
I couldn't agree more . . .
True. Yes, that's quite true . . .
I agree entirely . . .
I'm not sure. I quite agree . . .
All things considered, I must say that . . .
I'd like to say that I think that . . .
That's just what I was thinking.
You know, that's exactly what I think . . .
I agree entirely . . .
Well, you have a point there, but . . .

19. Expressing disagreement:

I disagree . . ./I would disagree with you.
That's not true.
You're wrong.
Impossible . . ./Nonsense . . . not allowed.
If you don't know . . .
I have got no idea . . .
I can't agree . . ./I don't agree . . .
That's not right . . ./I refuse . . .
That's all wrong . . .
I'm not with you . . ./Rubbish!
Ask somebody else . . .
Don't make me laugh.

Come off it.
I see things rather differently.

20. Expressing denial:

He denied all that he had said before.
That's not altogether true.
I do protest.
No, I never said that . . .
Nobody can affirm that . . .
Nothing can prove it.

21. Expressing speculation:

Just imagine if you became a millionaire . . .
Suppose you came into a lot of money. What would you
    do?
How would you feel about . . . ?
Oh, I suppose I'd . . .
Oh, I might . . .
Oh, I daresay I'd . . .
Oh, I expect I'd . . .

22. Expressing disbelief:

I can't believe it.
Rubbish! I don't believe it . . .
That's incredible . . .
You must be dreaming . . .
You must be joking . . .
That's the strangest thing I ever heard.
That's strange . . .
That's impossible/ridiculous.
Surely not.
Tell me what really happened.

23. Asking for and giving permission:

Please allow me to . . .
If you will allow me . . .
If no one objects . . .
You have my permission/leave to . . .
With your/his/her/permission . . .
May we smoke here?
Are we allowed to . . .?
Are we permitted to . . .?
Is it all right if we smoke in here?
Yes, you can/may.
Could/might we ask . . . ?
I wonder if I could/might . . .
Would you mind if I opened . . .
Would you mind my opening a window?
No, I don't mind at all.
No, not at all.

24. Expressing obligation:

You are obliged to . . ./It's obligatory . . .
You must be back by 2 o'clock.
You will have to be back . . .

You have to submit your work by . . .
I've got to finish . . . by tomorrow.
Need you work so hard?
Do you need to . . .?
Do you have to work hard?
We don't have to hurry.
I ought to phone . . .
I should phone . . .
You'd better be quick.
He'd better not make another mistake.
You may have to . . . You must/mustn't . . .
I have got to . . . Be sure to . . .
You are not allowed to . . .
It's your duty; you have got to . . .

25. Expressing prohibition:
I'm afraid they can't.
You mustn't keep us all waiting.
You oughtn't to waste money on . . .
He shouldn't be so impatient . . .
It's forbidden . . .
It's not allowed . . .

26. Expressing certainty/uncertainty (doubt):
I'm certain/sure that . . .
It's obvious/clear/plain that . . .
He has clearly/obviously/plainly/. . .
We don't doubt that he is honest . . .
Without doubt/doubtlessly . . .
They were uncertain/unsure of . . .
I doubt if/don't think . . .
We have doubts about his honesty.

27. Expressing probability:
It will probably rain today.
Perhaps it will rain.
It is likely that . . .
I suppose . . .

28. Expressing possibility/impossibility:
It is possible that . . .
It may be a good programme.
I think . . . (the book is in the bag).
It could be . . . (somewhere else).
The . . . could be anywhere.
It might be . . . Perhaps. I'm sure. I'm not sure.
He could have . . . . He might have . . .
Probably . . . They may . . ./might have been . . .
It is impossible (not possible) . . .
He can't have known the answer beforehand . . .

29. Asking for opinion:
What do you think of . . .?
What's your opinion . . .?
Do you think . . .?

30. Expressing warning:
Be careful . . . Look out . . . Mind the rush hour . . . Be
    aware of . . .
Don't . . . or else.
Be sure.
I'm warning you . . .
Always be careful . . .
Never take risks . . .
If I don't . . . I'll . . .
Wait and see . . . Look before you . . .
Don't you ever do that again.
This is my last word.
Don't go too far . . .
Think twice before you . . .
Watch out!
Never . . .
What you've got to remember is . . .

31. Expressing blame:
I blame you.
It's your fault.
How could you . . .
You should be careful . . .
You've got only yourself to blame.
You're always doing things like that.
You had to . . .
That's just like you.
That's no excuse.
I'm sorry to have to say this, but . . .

32. Release from blame:
It's OK.
Forget it.
Never mind. I don't mean it.
Don't worry . . .
That's all right.
It doesn't matter.
Give it a miss.
Things like that happen.
That's all right. All right.
It's all right.
It doesn't matter at all.
It wasn't your fault.
Oh it's not that important.
Forget it.

33. Expressing hope:
I hope so.
I do hope that . . .

34. Expressing preference:
I prefer . . .
I'd rather . . . than . . .
As far as I'm concerned . . .
To my mind . . .

I would like . . .
I prefer . . . to . . .
I like . . . more than . . .

35. Persuading people:
Can't I persuade you to . . .
Surely you can see . . .
Come on . . .
Please do come.
I'd love you to come.
It would be great if we could . . .
No, no, no; I insist on . . .
I forbid you to go . . .
You must understand . . .

36. Expressing gratitude:
We greatly appreciate your . . .
Thanks . . . , thank you very much.
I can't thank you enough.
I'm grateful to you . . .
I must thank you . . .
I'm much obliged.
Thank you very much indeed.
It's very kind of you . . .
I'll never forget you.

37. Expressing intention and aim:
I mean to . . ./intend to . . ./want to . . .
I have made up my mind.
I plan to . . ./propose to . . .
I have decided to . . ./I'm determined to . . .
She worked all out for/to . . .
It is vital . . ./important that we . . .
It is my intention to . . .
There are plans for me to . . .
What are your plans?
I'm going to . . .
I intend to . . .
I'm thinking of . . .
I'm definitely going to . . .
I may well . . .
I thought I might . . .

38. Advising/asking for advice:
I advise you . . .
My advice is . . .
The best thing for you to do is . . .
Make sure that you . . . Always make sure that . . .
Don't forget to . . .
Be sensible, don't . . .
You know it's not good for you . . .
Remember to . . .
If I were you . . .
If I were in your shoes . . .
If in doubt, don't . . .

Be very careful about . . .
You shouldn't . . .
What do you think (I should do)?
Would it be better to . . .?
I'd be better to . . .
Do you think it is wise . . .?
I wonder if you can help me . . .

39. Expressing anger:
Damn! Blast! Oh, hell!
I've had just about enough of your . . .
You stupid, bloody idiot!
Why the hell don't you . . .

40. Expressing sadness:
Oh God! What shall I do?
I can't take much more of this.
And as if that wasn't enough . . .

41. Cheering people up:
Come on!
It can't be as bad as all that.
Try and look on the bright side.

42. Asking about places:
Would you be so kind as to show me the way to . . .
Excuse me, could you . . .
Would you mind if . . .
I'd like you to . . .
Please will/would/could/you . . .
I'd like to know something about . . .

43. Invitation/inviting others to do something:
Would you like to have (dinner) with me?
What about going on a journey . . .
May I have the pleasure of . . .
What about a nice . . .
May I invite you to (supper) next . . .
How would you like to come and . . .?

44. Greeting people when meeting them:
Hello! Hi! Good morning/afternoon/evening.
Hello! How are you?
I'm very well, and how are you?

45. Greeting people when being introduced:
How do you do? Hallo! Hi!

46. Greeting people when leaving:
Goodbye, good night.
I'll see you tomorrow . . . next . . .
Bye-bye; cheerio; see you later.
So long, keep well.

47. Attracting attention:
Er, excuse me . . .
Er, I say . . .
Er, Mr . . .

48. Expressing refusal:
I'm awfully sorry, but . . .
You see . . . I'd like to say yes, but . . .
I can't really, because . . .

49. Expressing congratulations:
Congratulations . . .
I congratulate you . . .
My best wishes . . .
I wish you a happy . . .

50. Beginning a meal:
Help yourself to . . .
Help yourselves everybody . . .
What about more (soup)?
Yes, please.
No, thank you. I've had enough.

51. Encouraging people to do something:
Well done, now . . .
Right now . . .
Good. Fine.

52. Keeping going:
First of all you . . .
The first thing you have to do is . . .
The next thing you do is . . .
Oh, and by the way, don't forget to . . .
Make sure you remember to . . .
Oh, and be careful not to . . .
Hold on, I've forgotten to mention that . . .
I'm sorry, let me say that again.

53. Requesting:
Could you . . . ?
Would you please . . . ?
Would you mind . . .
Can . . . ?
Excuse me, can . . . ?
I wonder if you could . . .
Do you think you could . . .
Perhaps you can . . .
Would you be so kind as to . . .
Would you be kind enough to . . .

54. Guessing:
Perhaps . . . Possibly . . . Probably . . . Maybe . . .
It might be . . . It must be . . .
It could be . . . I'm not sure . . .
I guess . . . I know it's . . .

I think . . .
I suppose . . .

55. Asking for something:
Can I/May I/Could I have . . .
Could/Would you give me . . . please?
Have you got . . . ?
Do you think you could give me . . . please?
Would you mind giving me a . . . please?

56. Frequency:
Always; nearly always; usually; often; quite often;
    sometimes; rarely; almost never; never; once a
    day/week/month; twice a day/week/month; three
    times a day/week/month

57. Describing food:
Tasty; delicious; excellent; nice.

58. Offering assistance:
Let me . . .
I can . . . if you so wish.
I'll . . . if you like . . .
May/Can I help you?
May/Can I give you a hand?
Any help?
Can I be of any help to you?
Anything I can do for you?
I can save you the trouble, if you like.

59. Asking for assistance:
Can you help me, please?
Could you do me this favour?
Would you care to . . .

60. Responses to offering assistance:
Sure, certainly.
Of course, naturally.
By all means.
Sure if I can.
With pleasure; most willingly . . .
I don't mind at all.
I'm quite at your service.
I'm at your disposal.
With all my heart.
Oh, I'm sorry . . .
I'm afraid I can't.
Of course not.
Oh, I'm awfully sorry. It's none of my business.

61. Expressing judgement:
That ought to be rewarded.
Good work deserves good pay.
He certainly deserves to . . .
Must be rewarded/punished/praised.
Deserves to hold the name . . .

62. Expressing duration:
How long?
I've been . . . since/for. . .
I have been playing chess for six years.

63. Expressing sensation:
It tastes/smells awful/delicious/horrible.
It sounds . . .
It feels . . .
It looks

64. Asking questions for continuing conversation:
What happened next . . .?
Had you already . . .?
Have you ever . . .?
Didn't you once . . .?
Can you remember . . .?
What were you saying?

65. Explaining ideas:
In my opinion . . .
I think that . . .
In the first place . . .
Secondly . . .
On the other hand . . .
However, . . .
For example, . . .
In general . . .

66. Expressing sympathy:
How sad . . ./terrible/awful . . .
Poor . . . (person's name).
I was so sorry to hear . . .

I cannot tell you how sorry I was . . .
I was shocked to hear . . .
I'm sorry . . .

67. Expressing comparison:
It's like . . . . It looks like . . .
More than . . . . Less than . . . The most . . .
They match . . . They don't match.
They are similar. They aren't similar
The similarities are . . .

68. Answering techniques:
Well, let me see . . .
Well, now . . .
Oh, let me think for moment . . .
I'm not sure, I'll just have to find out
I'm glad you asked me that

69. Avoiding answering altogether:
I'd rather not answer that, if you don't mind.
I'm terribly sorry, I really don't know.
I've no idea, I'm afraid.
I can't answer that one.

70. Reporting:
He said that . . . He told . . .
He wondered . . .
She tried to find out . . .
She started commenting that . . .
I found out that . . .
They went on to say that . . .
Anyway, to cut a long story short . . .
It's all coming back to me now.

Bibliography

Andrew C O   1980   *Testing Language Ability in the Classroom.* Newbury House, Rowley, Mass.

Alexander L G   1976   Where do we go from here? A reconsideration affecting course design. *ELT*, 30, 2

Altas J E *et al.* (eds)   1981   *The Second Language Classroom.* OUP

Bowen J D and Stockwell S R   1968   *Forward to Modern English Language Learning*, Vol. 7

Bright M   1973   *Teaching English as a Second Language.* Longman

Bright J A and Piggot R   1976   *Handwriting.* Cambridge University Press, England

Brumfit C J   1980   *Problems and Principles in English Teaching.* Pergamon, Oxford

Brumfit C J   1979   *The Communicative Approach to Language Teaching.* OUP

Bung K   1973   *The Specifications of Objectives in a Language Learning System for Adults.* Strasbourg: Council of Europe

Caroll J B   1968   *The Study of Language.* Cambridge, Harvard University Press

Chomsky N   1965   *Aspects of the Theory of Syntax.* Cambridge, MIT

Chomsky N   1957   *Syntactic Structures.* The Hague, Mouton and Co.

Clark C R   1980   *Language Teaching Techniques.* Pro Lingua Associates, Vermont, USA

Clark L H and Starr L S   1967   *Secondary School Teaching Methods.* 2nd ed. Macmillan, New York

Clark H and Clark E   1977   *Psychology and Language.* Harcourt, Brace and Jovanovich, New York

Close R A   1968   *English as a Foreign Language.* George Allen and Unwin, London

Cohen D A   1980   *Testing Language Ability in the Classroom.* Newbury House, Rowley, Mass.

Collins V H   1961   *A Book of English Idioms.* Longman

Dacanay F R   1967   *Techniques and Procedures in Second Language Teaching.* Oceana Publications, New York

Davis A (ed.)   1968   *Language Testing Symposium: A Psycholinguistic Approach.* OUP

Diller C   1978   *The Language Teaching Controversy.* Newbury House, Rowley, Mass.

Dobson J M   1979   'The notional syllabus: theory and practice'. *FORUM*, 17, 2

El-Araby S   1974   *Audio-Visual Aids for Teaching English.* Longman

Finocchiaro M   1979   The functional-notional syllabus: promise, problems, practices. *FORUM*, 17, 2

Finocchiaro M and Brumfit C 1973   *Functional Notional Approach: From Theory to Practice.* OUP

Fries C C   1957   *The Structure of English.* Longman

Gardner R and Lambert W   1972   *Attitudes and Motivation in Second Language Learning.* Newbury House, Rowley, Mass.

Goodman K S   1967   Reading: A Psycholinguistic Guessing Game, in Gunderson, D.V., *Language and Reading.* Washington, D.C. Publishers

Halliday M A K   1973   *Explorations in the function of language.* Edward Arnold, London

Harris D P   1969   *Testing English as a Second Language.* McGraw Hill, New York

Harsh W   1975   'Three approaches: traditional grammar; descriptive linguistics and generative grammar'. *The Art of TESOL, Part (1)*, *FORUM*, Washington, D.C.

Haycraft J   1978   *An Introduction to English Language Teaching.* Longman

Hornby A S   1962   *The Teaching of Structural Word and Sentence Patterns.* OUP

Hwang J R   1970   Current trends of language learning and teaching. *FORUM*, Vol. 8, 2

Hymes D M   1964   *Language in Culture and Society.* Dell (*ed.*). Harper and Row, New York

Jespersen O   1969   *Analytic Syntax.* Holt, Rinehart and Winston, Inc., New York

Johnson K   1981   *Communicate in Writing.* Longman, London

Joycey E   1983   Finalizing the preparation of a lesson. *FORUM*, Vol. 21, No. 2

Krashen S   1981   *Second Language Acquisition and Second Language Learning.* Pergamon Press, Oxford

Krashen S and Terrell B T (eds)   1983   *The Natural Approach.* Pergamon Press, Oxford

Lado R   1961   *Language Testing.* McGraw Hill, New York

Lado R   1964   *Language Teaching: A Scientific Approach.* McGraw Hill, New York

Lee W R   1965   *Language Teaching: Games and Contests.* OUP

Leech G N and Svartvik J   1975   *Communicative Grammar of English.* Longman

Levine J   1972   Creating Environments for Developing Communicative Competence. Publications of Lancaster University, England

Lewis M and Hill J   1985   *Practical Techniques for Language Teaching.* Language Teaching Publications, England

Littlewood W   1981   *Communicative Language Learning: An Introduction.* Cambridge University Press

Lyons J   1968   *Introduction to Theoretical Linguistics.* Cambridge University Press

Macintosh H G   1974   *Techniques and Problems of Assessment.* Edward Arnold, London

Madsen S H   1983   *Techniques in Testing.* OUP

Morrow K   1979   'Communicative language testing: revolution or evolution?' In Brumfit and Johnson's, *The Communicative Approach to Language Teaching.* OUP

Morgan J and Rinvolucri M   1985   *Vocabulary.* OUP

Moulton W   1961   Linguistics and Language Teaching in the United States 1940–1960 in Mohrmann, Sommerfelt, and Whatmough, pp. 86–89

Munby J   1978   *Communicative Syllabus Design.* Cambridge University Press

Nasr R T   1963   *The Teaching of English to Arab Students.* Longman, London

Oller J W Jr   1979   *Language Tests at School.* Longman, London

Pride J B and Holness J (eds)   1972   *Penguin Modern Linguistics Readings.* Penguin

Raimes A   1983   *Techniques in Teaching Writing.* OUP

Revel J   1983   *Teaching Techniques for Communicative English.* Macmillan

Richterich R   1971   *Identifying the Needs of Adults Learning a Foreign Language*. Pergamon Press, Oxford

Rivers W   1972   *Teaching Foreign-Language Skills*. The University of Chicago Press, London, Second Edition 1981

Rivers W   1972   *Speaking in Many Tongues*. Newbury House, Rowley, Mass.

Rivers W   1983   *Communicating Naturally in a Second Language*. Harvard University Press

Roberts P   1962   *English Sentences*. Harcourt, Brace and World, New York

Robinett W   1978   *Teaching English to Speakers of Other Languages*. McGraw Hill, New York

Robinson N G   1985   *Crosscultural Understanding*. Pergamon Press, Oxford

Roulet E   1972   *Linguistics Theory, Linguistic Description and Language Teaching*. Translation by Candlin, C.N., Longman, London

Savignon S J   1983   *Communicative Competence: Theory and Classroom Practice*. Reading, Mass.

Skinner C E   1959   *Educational Psychology*. 4th ed., Prentice Hall, Englewood Cliffs

Smith H P   1962   *Psychology in Teaching*. 2nd ed., Prentice Hall, Englewood Cliffs

Spencer D H   1967   *Guided Composition Exercises*. Longman, London

Stratton F   1977   Putting the communicative syllabus in its place. *TESOL Quarterly* 11, 2

Swan M   1985   A critical look at the communicative approach. *ELT*, 93, 1 and 2

Trim J   1973   *Draft Outline of a European Unit-Credit System for Modern Language-Learning by Adults*. Strasbourg: The Council for Cultural Co-operation of the Council of Europe

Ur P   1984   *Teaching Listening Comprehension*. CUP

Vallette R M   1969   *Directions in Foreign Language Testing*. Modern Language Association, New York

Vallette R M   1977   *Modern Language Testing: A Handbook*. 2nd ed., Harcourt Brace Jovanovich, New York

Walkwork J F   1969   *Language and Linguistics*. Heinemann, London

Widdowson H G   1978   *Teaching Language as Communication*. OUP

Wilkins D A   1972   *Linguistics in Language Teaching*. Edward Arnold, London

Wilkins D   1976   *Notional Syllabuses*. OUP, London

Wright A   1976   *Visual Materials for the Language Teacher*. Longman, London

Index

This index covers all chapters and Appendix I (not Appendix II or the bibliography). The alphabetical order is word-by-word: a group of letters followed by a space, a hypen, or a dash, comes before the same group of letters followed immediately by another letter, so 'multi-word verbs' files before 'multiple-choice exercises'.